50 Premium Canadian Bread Recipes for Home

By: Kelly Johnson

Table of Contents

- Classic Canadian Bannock
- Maple Walnut Bread
- Montreal Style Bagels
- Canadian Rye Bread
- Buttermilk Biscuits
- Nanaimo Bar Bread
- Canadian Oatmeal Bread
- Quebecois Pumpernickel
- Canadian Wheat Bread
- Lemon Blueberry Scones
- Maple Pecan Loaf
- Saskatoon Berry Bread
- Wild Rice Bread
- Canadian Cheddar Chive Bread
- Buttermilk Cornbread
- Timothy Hay Bread
- Nova Scotia Brown Bread
- Montreal Rye with Caraway Seeds
- Cinnamon Raisin Swirl Bread
- Canadian Honey Whole Wheat Bread
- Maple Raisin Bread
- Spelt and Flaxseed Bread
- Prairie Seed Bread
- Canadian Fruit and Nut Bread
- Rosemary Garlic Focaccia
- Dandelion Greens Bread
- Vancouver Island Herb Bread
- Traditional Bannock with Lard
- Honey Oat Loaf
- Maple Glazed Brioche
- Pumpkin Seed Rye Bread
- Cornmeal Muffins

- Sour Cherry Rye Bread
- Cranberry Orange Bread
- Canadian Caramelized Onion Bread
- Herb and Cheese Pull-Apart Bread
- Wild Berry Buttermilk Muffins
- Alberta Grain Bread
- Lemon Poppy Seed Loaf
- Canadian Bacon and Cheese Bread
- Saskatoon Berry and Almond Bread
- Maple-Glazed Pretzel Bites
- Flaxseed and Sunflower Seed Bread
- Crusty Canadian White Bread
- Oat and Wheat Sandwich Bread
- Cheddar and Jalapeno Bread
- Maple Apple Cinnamon Bread
- Flavored Bannock Bread
- Wild Mushroom Rye Bread
- Vancouver Island Gingerbread

Classic Canadian Bannock

Ingredients:

- 2 cups (250 g) all-purpose flour
- 1 tablespoon (15 g) baking powder
- 1 teaspoon (5 g) salt
- 1/4 cup (50 g) sugar (optional, for a slightly sweet version)
- 1/4 cup (60 g) unsalted butter or lard, chilled and cut into small pieces
- 3/4 cup (180 ml) milk (you can also use water or buttermilk)
- 1 large egg (optional, for a richer dough)

Instructions:

1. **Preheat Oven (if baking):**
   - Preheat your oven to 400°F (200°C). Grease a baking sheet or line it with parchment paper.
2. **Mix Dry Ingredients:**
   - In a large mixing bowl, whisk together the flour, baking powder, salt, and sugar (if using).
3. **Cut in Fat:**
   - Add the chilled butter or lard to the dry ingredients. Use a pastry cutter, fork, or your fingers to cut the fat into the flour mixture until it resembles coarse crumbs.
4. **Add Wet Ingredients:**
   - If using, beat the egg and add it to the milk. Pour the milk (and egg mixture) into the dry ingredients. Stir until just combined. The dough should be somewhat sticky but manageable.
5. **Shape the Dough:**
   - Turn the dough out onto a lightly floured surface. Gently knead the dough a few times until it comes together. Pat it into a round or rectangle shape, about 1/2 inch (1.25 cm) thick.
6. **Cooking Methods:**
   - **Baking:** Place the shaped dough on the prepared baking sheet. Bake for 20-25 minutes, or until the top is golden brown and the bread sounds hollow when tapped.
   - **Frying:** Heat a skillet over medium heat and add a small amount of oil or butter. Fry the dough, cooking each side for 3-5 minutes, until golden brown and cooked through.
   - **Campfire:** Place the dough on a greased cast iron skillet or directly on a campfire grill. Cook over medium heat, turning occasionally, until the bannock is golden brown and cooked through.
7. **Cool and Serve:**

- Allow the bannock to cool slightly before slicing. Serve warm with butter, jam, or your favorite toppings.

Notes:

- **Flavors:** You can customize bannock by adding ingredients like herbs, cheese, or dried fruit to the dough.
- **Consistency:** Adjust the amount of liquid as needed to get the right dough consistency. It should be moist but not too sticky.
- **Storage:** Bannock can be stored at room temperature for a few days, or frozen for longer storage.

Enjoy your Classic Canadian Bannock! This simple and hearty bread is perfect for breakfast, snacks, or as an accompaniment to soups and stews.

Maple Walnut Bread

Ingredients:

- **For the Dough:**
    - 3 ½ cups (440 g) all-purpose flour
    - 1 cup (120 g) whole wheat flour
    - 1/3 cup (80 ml) pure maple syrup
    - 1 cup (240 ml) warm milk (110°F or 45°C)
    - 2 teaspoons (6 g) active dry yeast
    - 1 teaspoon (5 g) salt
    - 1/4 cup (60 g) unsalted butter, softened
    - 1 large egg
    - 1 cup (120 g) toasted walnuts, chopped
- **For the Topping (optional):**
    - 2 tablespoons maple syrup (for glazing)
    - Extra chopped walnuts (for sprinkling)

Instructions:

1. **Prepare the Yeast:**
    - In a small bowl, dissolve the maple syrup in the warm milk. Sprinkle the yeast over the surface and let it sit for 5-10 minutes, or until it becomes frothy and bubbly.
2. **Mix the Dough:**
    - In a large mixing bowl, combine the all-purpose flour, whole wheat flour, and salt.
    - Make a well in the center and add the yeast mixture, softened butter, and egg.
    - Stir until a rough dough forms. Fold in the chopped toasted walnuts.
3. **Knead the Dough:**
    - Turn the dough out onto a lightly floured surface and knead for about 8-10 minutes, or until it becomes smooth and elastic. The dough should be slightly tacky but manageable.
4. **First Rise:**
    - Place the dough in a lightly greased bowl and cover it with plastic wrap or a damp cloth.
    - Let it rise in a warm place for about 1-1.5 hours, or until it has doubled in size.
5. **Shape the Bread:**
    - Punch down the risen dough to release air. Turn it out onto a lightly floured surface.
    - Shape the dough into a loaf or divide it into smaller rolls, depending on your preference.
    - Place the shaped loaf on a parchment-lined baking sheet or in a greased loaf pan.

6. **Second Rise:**
   - Cover the shaped loaf with plastic wrap or a damp cloth and let it rise for another 30-45 minutes, or until it has risen noticeably.
7. **Preheat Oven:**
   - Preheat your oven to 375°F (190°C).
8. **Prepare for Baking:**
   - If desired, brush the top of the loaf with additional maple syrup and sprinkle with extra chopped walnuts for added texture and flavor.
9. **Bake:**
   - Bake in the preheated oven for 30-35 minutes, or until the bread is golden brown and sounds hollow when tapped on the bottom.
10. **Cool:**
    - Remove the bread from the oven and let it cool in the pan for about 10 minutes before transferring it to a wire rack to cool completely.

Notes:

- **Maple Syrup:** Use pure maple syrup for the best flavor. The maple syrup not only sweetens the bread but also gives it a lovely aroma.
- **Walnuts:** Toasting the walnuts enhances their flavor. To toast, spread them on a baking sheet and bake at 350°F (175°C) for 8-10 minutes, or until fragrant and lightly browned.
- **Texture:** The bread will have a slightly sweet and nutty flavor, with a tender crumb and a slightly crisp crust.

Enjoy your Maple Walnut Bread! It's a delightful combination of sweet maple syrup and crunchy walnuts, perfect for a special breakfast or as a snack throughout the day.

Montreal Style Bagels

Ingredients:

- **For the Bagels:**
    - 4 cups (500 g) all-purpose flour
    - 1 ½ teaspoons (9 g) salt
    - 1 tablespoon (15 g) sugar
    - 1 tablespoon (15 g) active dry yeast
    - 1 ¼ cups (300 ml) warm water (110°F or 45°C)
    - 2 tablespoons (30 ml) honey (for the dough)
    - 1 egg, beaten (for egg wash)
    - Sesame seeds or poppy seeds (for topping)
- **For the Boiling Water:**
    - 2 quarts (2 liters) water
    - 2 tablespoons (30 ml) honey

Instructions:

1. **Prepare the Yeast:**
    - In a small bowl, dissolve the sugar in the warm water. Sprinkle the yeast over the surface and let it sit for 5-10 minutes, or until it becomes frothy and bubbly.
2. **Mix the Dough:**
    - In a large mixing bowl, combine the flour and salt.
    - Make a well in the center and add the yeast mixture and honey.
    - Stir until a rough dough forms. The dough should be somewhat stiff.
3. **Knead the Dough:**
    - Turn the dough out onto a lightly floured surface and knead for about 8-10 minutes, or until it becomes smooth and elastic. The dough will be slightly sticky but manageable.
4. **First Rise:**
    - Place the dough in a lightly greased bowl and cover it with plastic wrap or a damp cloth.
    - Let it rise in a warm place for about 1 hour, or until it has doubled in size.
5. **Shape the Bagels:**
    - Punch down the risen dough and turn it out onto a lightly floured surface.
    - Divide the dough into 12-16 equal pieces, depending on your preferred size.
    - Roll each piece into a ball and then use your thumb to poke a hole in the center, stretching the dough to form a ring. The hole should be about 1-2 inches (2.5-5 cm) wide.
6. **Prepare for Boiling:**
    - In a large pot, bring 2 quarts of water to a boil. Add 2 tablespoons of honey to the water.

- Carefully drop the bagels into the boiling water, a few at a time, and boil for about 1-2 minutes on each side. This step helps to develop the bagels' chewy texture.
7. **Preheat Oven:**
    - Preheat your oven to 425°F (220°C). Line a baking sheet with parchment paper or a silicone baking mat.
8. **Bake the Bagels:**
    - Remove the bagels from the boiling water and place them on the prepared baking sheet.
    - Brush the tops with the beaten egg and sprinkle with sesame seeds or poppy seeds, if desired.
    - Bake in the preheated oven for 15-20 minutes, or until the bagels are golden brown and have a slightly crisp crust.
9. **Cool:**
    - Allow the bagels to cool on a wire rack before slicing.

Notes:

- **Honey in Boiling Water:** Adding honey to the boiling water gives the bagels a slightly sweet flavor and contributes to their shiny, crisp crust.
- **Size of Bagels:** Montreal-style bagels are typically smaller and denser than New York-style bagels. Adjust the size according to your preference.
- **Toppings:** Traditional toppings include sesame seeds or poppy seeds, but you can also experiment with other toppings like coarse salt, garlic, or onion flakes.

Enjoy your homemade Montreal-style bagels! They are perfect for sandwiches, with cream cheese, or simply enjoyed on their own.

Canadian Rye Bread

Ingredients:

- **For the Dough:**
    - 1 ½ cups (180 g) rye flour
    - 2 ½ cups (310 g) all-purpose flour
    - 1 tablespoon (15 g) sugar
    - 1 ½ teaspoons (9 g) salt
    - 2 teaspoons (6 g) active dry yeast
    - 1 ½ cups (360 ml) warm water (110°F or 45°C)
    - 2 tablespoons (30 ml) vegetable oil or melted butter
    - 1 tablespoon (15 ml) caraway seeds (optional)
    - 1 tablespoon (15 ml) molasses (optional, for a deeper flavor)
- **For the Topping (optional):**
    - 1 tablespoon caraway seeds or coarse salt

Instructions:

1. **Prepare the Yeast:**
    - In a small bowl, dissolve the sugar in the warm water. Sprinkle the yeast over the surface and let it sit for 5-10 minutes, or until it becomes frothy and bubbly.
2. **Mix the Dough:**
    - In a large mixing bowl, combine the rye flour, all-purpose flour, and salt.
    - Make a well in the center and add the yeast mixture, vegetable oil (or melted butter), and molasses (if using).
    - Stir until a rough dough forms. Fold in the caraway seeds if you're using them.
3. **Knead the Dough:**
    - Turn the dough out onto a lightly floured surface and knead for about 8-10 minutes, or until it becomes smooth and elastic. Rye dough is denser and can be stickier than wheat dough, so you may need to adjust the flour as needed.
4. **First Rise:**
    - Place the dough in a lightly greased bowl and cover it with plastic wrap or a damp cloth.
    - Let it rise in a warm place for about 1-1.5 hours, or until it has doubled in size.
5. **Shape the Bread:**
    - Punch down the risen dough to release air. Turn it out onto a lightly floured surface.
    - Shape the dough into a loaf by flattening it into a rectangle and rolling it up tightly from one edge to the other. Alternatively, you can shape it into a round loaf.
    - Place the shaped loaf into a greased 9x5 inch (23x13 cm) loaf pan or onto a parchment-lined baking sheet.
6. **Second Rise:**

- Cover the shaped loaf with plastic wrap or a damp cloth and let it rise for another 30-45 minutes, or until it has risen noticeably.
7. **Preheat Oven:**
    - Preheat your oven to 375°F (190°C).
8. **Prepare for Baking:**
    - If desired, sprinkle the top of the loaf with additional caraway seeds or coarse salt for added flavor and texture.
    - Use a sharp knife to make a few slashes on top of the loaf to allow for expansion.
9. **Bake:**
    - Bake in the preheated oven for 30-35 minutes, or until the bread is golden brown and sounds hollow when tapped on the bottom.
10. **Cool:**
    - Remove the bread from the oven and let it cool in the pan for about 10 minutes before transferring it to a wire rack to cool completely.

Notes:

- **Rye Flour:** Rye flour gives the bread its distinctive flavor and texture. For a lighter loaf, you can use a higher proportion of all-purpose flour.
- **Molasses:** Adding molasses enhances the flavor and color of the bread. You can omit it for a lighter taste.
- **Texture:** Rye bread has a denser crumb and a slightly more chewy texture compared to wheat bread. This is characteristic of traditional rye breads.

Enjoy your Canadian Rye Bread! It's perfect for sandwiches, with a smear of butter, or as a hearty accompaniment to soups and stews.

Buttermilk Biscuits

Ingredients:

- 2 cups (250 g) all-purpose flour
- 1 tablespoon (15 g) baking powder
- ½ teaspoon (2.5 g) baking soda
- 1 teaspoon (5 g) salt
- 1/4 cup (50 g) granulated sugar (optional, for slightly sweet biscuits)
- 1/2 cup (115 g) cold unsalted butter, cut into small pieces
- 1 cup (240 ml) cold buttermilk
- 1 large egg (optional, for brushing on top)

Instructions:

1. **Preheat Oven:**
   - Preheat your oven to 425°F (220°C). Line a baking sheet with parchment paper or a silicone baking mat.
2. **Mix Dry Ingredients:**
   - In a large mixing bowl, whisk together the flour, baking powder, baking soda, salt, and sugar (if using).
3. **Cut in the Butter:**
   - Add the cold, cubed butter to the dry ingredients. Using a pastry cutter, fork, or your fingers, cut the butter into the flour mixture until it resembles coarse crumbs with pea-sized pieces of butter.
4. **Add Buttermilk:**
   - Make a well in the center of the dry ingredients and pour in the cold buttermilk.
   - Stir gently with a wooden spoon or spatula until just combined. The dough will be slightly sticky.
5. **Turn Out and Pat the Dough:**
   - Turn the dough out onto a lightly floured surface. Gently pat it into a rectangle or square about 1-inch (2.5 cm) thick. Avoid overworking the dough to keep the biscuits tender.
6. **Cut the Biscuits:**
   - Using a floured biscuit cutter (about 2-3 inches in diameter), cut out biscuits from the dough. Press straight down without twisting to ensure the biscuits rise evenly.
   - Gather any leftover dough, gently re-pat it, and cut out additional biscuits.
7. **Prepare for Baking:**
   - Place the cut biscuits onto the prepared baking sheet, placing them close together for soft sides or spaced apart for crispier edges.
   - If desired, brush the tops with a beaten egg for a golden, glossy finish.
8. **Bake:**

- Bake in the preheated oven for 12-15 minutes, or until the biscuits are golden brown and cooked through.
9. **Cool and Serve:**
    - Remove the biscuits from the oven and let them cool slightly on a wire rack before serving.

Notes:

- **Butter:** For best results, keep the butter and buttermilk as cold as possible. This helps create a flaky texture.
- **Handling Dough:** Be gentle with the dough to avoid overworking it, which can lead to dense biscuits.
- **Biscuits Cutter:** If you don't have a biscuit cutter, you can use the rim of a glass or jar. Just make sure to flour the edges to prevent sticking.

Enjoy your Buttermilk Biscuits fresh out of the oven with butter, jam, honey, or as an accompaniment to your favorite meal!

Nanaimo Bar Bread

Ingredients:

- **For the Bread:**
    - 3 cups (375 g) all-purpose flour
    - ¼ cup (50 g) granulated sugar
    - 1 tablespoon (15 g) baking powder
    - ½ teaspoon (2.5 g) salt
    - ½ cup (115 g) unsalted butter, cold and cut into small pieces
    - 1 cup (240 ml) milk
    - 2 large eggs
    - 1 teaspoon (5 ml) vanilla extract
    - 1 cup (150 g) semi-sweet chocolate chips
    - 1 cup (150 g) chopped walnuts (optional)
- **For the Custard Filling:**
    - ½ cup (100 g) granulated sugar
    - ¼ cup (30 g) instant vanilla pudding mix
    - ¼ cup (60 ml) milk
- **For the Topping (optional):**
    - ½ cup (90 g) semi-sweet chocolate chips, melted
    - 1 tablespoon (10 g) graham cracker crumbs

Instructions:

1. **Prepare the Custard Filling:**
    - In a small bowl, whisk together the granulated sugar, instant vanilla pudding mix, and milk until smooth and slightly thickened. Set aside.
2. **Preheat Oven:**
    - Preheat your oven to 350°F (175°C). Grease a 9x5 inch (23x13 cm) loaf pan or line it with parchment paper.
3. **Mix Dry Ingredients:**
    - In a large bowl, combine the flour, sugar, baking powder, and salt. Mix well.
4. **Cut in the Butter:**
    - Add the cold, cubed butter to the flour mixture. Using a pastry cutter, fork, or your fingers, cut the butter into the flour until it resembles coarse crumbs.
5. **Add Wet Ingredients:**
    - In a separate bowl, whisk together the milk, eggs, and vanilla extract. Pour this mixture into the dry ingredients.
    - Stir until just combined. The dough will be thick and somewhat sticky. Fold in the chocolate chips and chopped walnuts (if using).
6. **Assemble the Bread:**
    - Spread half of the dough evenly in the prepared loaf pan.

- Spoon the custard filling over the dough, spreading it out evenly.
- Top with the remaining dough, spreading it gently over the custard layer. It's okay if some custard shows through.

7. **Bake:**
   - Bake in the preheated oven for 50-60 minutes, or until a toothpick inserted into the center comes out clean and the top is golden brown.

8. **Prepare the Topping (Optional):**
   - While the bread is baking, melt the remaining chocolate chips in a microwave-safe bowl or over a double boiler. Drizzle the melted chocolate over the cooled bread.
   - Sprinkle with graham cracker crumbs for a finishing touch.

9. **Cool and Slice:**
   - Allow the bread to cool in the pan for about 10 minutes before transferring to a wire rack to cool completely.
   - Once cooled, slice and enjoy!

Notes:

- **Custard Filling:** The custard filling adds a creamy layer reminiscent of the classic Nanaimo bar. Ensure it's well-spread to maintain even layers.
- **Texture:** The bread has a tender crumb with a touch of sweetness and chocolatey goodness, enhanced by the custard layer.
- **Serving:** This bread is great for breakfast, as a snack, or even as a dessert. It pairs wonderfully with a cup of tea or coffee.

Enjoy your Nanaimo Bar Bread! It combines the beloved flavors of the Nanaimo bar into a unique and satisfying bread.

Canadian Oatmeal Bread

Ingredients:

- **For the Bread:**
    - 1 cup (90 g) rolled oats
    - 1 ½ cups (360 ml) water
    - 1/3 cup (80 ml) milk
    - 2 tablespoons (30 g) unsalted butter
    - 1 tablespoon (15 g) granulated sugar
    - 2 teaspoons (6 g) active dry yeast
    - 3 ½ cups (440 g) all-purpose flour
    - 1 teaspoon (5 g) salt
    - 1 large egg
- **For the Topping (optional):**
    - 2 tablespoons rolled oats
    - 1 tablespoon honey or melted butter (for brushing)

Instructions:

1. **Prepare the Oats:**
    - In a medium saucepan, bring the 1 ½ cups of water to a boil. Stir in the rolled oats, reduce the heat, and simmer for 5 minutes, or until the oats are soft and have absorbed most of the water. Remove from heat and let cool slightly.
2. **Mix Wet Ingredients:**
    - In a small saucepan, heat the milk and butter over low heat until the butter is melted. Remove from heat and let cool until it is warm but not hot (110°F or 45°C).
3. **Prepare the Yeast:**
    - In a small bowl, dissolve the sugar in the warm milk mixture. Sprinkle the yeast over the surface and let it sit for 5-10 minutes, or until it becomes frothy and bubbly.
4. **Mix the Dough:**
    - In a large mixing bowl, combine the flour and salt. Make a well in the center and add the yeast mixture, cooked oats, and the egg.
    - Stir until the dough begins to come together. You may need to add a little more flour or water to achieve a soft, slightly sticky dough.
5. **Knead the Dough:**
    - Turn the dough out onto a lightly floured surface and knead for about 8-10 minutes, or until it becomes smooth and elastic. The dough should be slightly tacky but manageable.
6. **First Rise:**

- Place the dough in a lightly greased bowl and cover it with plastic wrap or a damp cloth.
- Let it rise in a warm place for about 1-1.5 hours, or until it has doubled in size.

7. **Shape the Bread:**
   - Punch down the risen dough and turn it out onto a lightly floured surface. Shape the dough into a loaf by flattening it into a rectangle and rolling it up tightly from one edge to the other.
   - Place the shaped loaf into a greased 9x5 inch (23x13 cm) loaf pan.

8. **Second Rise:**
   - Cover the loaf with plastic wrap or a damp cloth and let it rise for another 30-45 minutes, or until it has risen noticeably.

9. **Preheat Oven:**
   - Preheat your oven to 375°F (190°C).

10. **Prepare for Baking:**
    - If desired, brush the top of the loaf with honey or melted butter and sprinkle with additional rolled oats.

11. **Bake:**
    - Bake in the preheated oven for 30-35 minutes, or until the bread is golden brown and sounds hollow when tapped on the bottom.

12. **Cool:**
    - Allow the bread to cool in the pan for about 10 minutes before transferring it to a wire rack to cool completely.

Notes:

- **Oats:** Use rolled oats for the best texture. Instant or quick oats can be used but may change the texture slightly.
- **Texture:** This bread has a hearty, chewy texture thanks to the oats, and it's great for toasting or as a base for hearty sandwiches.
- **Storage:** Store the cooled bread in an airtight container at room temperature for up to 4-5 days, or freeze for longer storage.

Enjoy your homemade Canadian Oatmeal Bread! It's nutritious, delicious, and perfect for any time of day.

Quebecois Pumpernickel

Ingredients:

- **For the Dough:**
    - 1 cup (240 ml) warm water (110°F or 45°C)
    - 1 tablespoon (15 g) active dry yeast
    - 1 tablespoon (15 g) granulated sugar
    - 1 cup (125 g) rye flour
    - 1 cup (125 g) whole wheat flour
    - 1 cup (125 g) all-purpose flour
    - 1/4 cup (60 ml) molasses
    - 2 tablespoons (30 g) unsalted butter, melted
    - 1 teaspoon (5 g) salt
    - 1 tablespoon (15 g) caraway seeds (optional, for traditional flavor)
    - 1/2 cup (50 g) finely chopped walnuts or sunflower seeds (optional, for added texture)
- **For the Topping (optional):**
    - 1 tablespoon caraway seeds
    - 1 tablespoon all-purpose flour (to dust)

Instructions:

1. **Prepare the Yeast:**
    - In a small bowl, combine the warm water, sugar, and yeast. Stir and let sit for about 5-10 minutes, or until the mixture becomes frothy and bubbly.
2. **Mix the Dry Ingredients:**
    - In a large mixing bowl, combine the rye flour, whole wheat flour, and all-purpose flour. If using caraway seeds, add them to the dry ingredients.
3. **Combine Wet Ingredients:**
    - Add the molasses, melted butter, and salt to the yeast mixture. Stir to combine.
4. **Mix the Dough:**
    - Make a well in the center of the dry ingredients and pour in the yeast mixture. Stir until a rough dough forms.
    - Add the chopped walnuts or sunflower seeds if using, and stir to combine.
5. **Knead the Dough:**
    - Turn the dough out onto a lightly floured surface and knead for about 8-10 minutes, or until the dough is smooth and elastic. The dough will be dense but should be manageable.
6. **First Rise:**
    - Place the dough in a lightly greased bowl and cover it with plastic wrap or a damp cloth. Let it rise in a warm place for about 1-1.5 hours, or until it has doubled in size.
7. **Shape the Loaf:**
    - Punch down the risen dough and turn it out onto a floured surface. Shape the dough into a loaf by flattening it slightly and then rolling it up tightly. Alternatively, shape it into a round loaf.

8. **Second Rise:**
   - Place the shaped dough into a greased 9x5 inch (23x13 cm) loaf pan or onto a parchment-lined baking sheet. Cover it with plastic wrap or a damp cloth and let it rise for another 30-45 minutes, or until it has risen noticeably.
9. **Preheat Oven:**
   - Preheat your oven to 375°F (190°C).
10. **Prepare for Baking:**
    - If desired, dust the top of the loaf with a bit of all-purpose flour and sprinkle with additional caraway seeds for a traditional touch.
11. **Bake:**
    - Bake in the preheated oven for 35-40 minutes, or until the bread is deep brown and sounds hollow when tapped on the bottom.
12. **Cool:**
    - Allow the bread to cool in the pan for about 10 minutes before transferring it to a wire rack to cool completely.

Notes:

- **Texture and Flavor:** Pumpernickel bread is typically dense and moist. The molasses adds a touch of sweetness and deepens the color of the bread.
- **Variations:** For a more authentic Quebecois touch, consider incorporating local ingredients or variations in spices based on regional preferences.

Enjoy your Quebecois Pumpernickel Bread! It pairs wonderfully with hearty soups, cheese, or simply a pat of butter.

Canadian Wheat Bread

Ingredients:

- **For the Dough:**
    - 2 ½ cups (320 g) whole wheat flour
    - 1 ½ cups (190 g) all-purpose flour
    - ¼ cup (50 g) granulated sugar or honey
    - 1 tablespoon (15 g) active dry yeast
    - 1 ½ teaspoons (9 g) salt
    - 1 ½ cups (360 ml) warm water (110°F or 45°C)
    - ¼ cup (60 ml) vegetable oil or melted butter
    - 1 large egg
- **For the Topping (optional):**
    - 1 tablespoon rolled oats or wheat bran (for sprinkling on top)

Instructions:

1. **Prepare the Yeast:**
    - In a small bowl, dissolve the sugar or honey in the warm water. Sprinkle the yeast over the surface and let it sit for 5-10 minutes, or until it becomes frothy and bubbly.
2. **Mix Dry Ingredients:**
    - In a large mixing bowl, combine the whole wheat flour, all-purpose flour, and salt. Mix well.
3. **Combine Wet Ingredients:**
    - In a separate bowl, whisk together the egg and vegetable oil (or melted butter).
4. **Mix the Dough:**
    - Make a well in the center of the dry ingredients and pour in the yeast mixture and the egg mixture.
    - Stir until the dough begins to come together. You may need to adjust the amount of flour or water slightly to achieve a soft, slightly sticky dough.
5. **Knead the Dough:**
    - Turn the dough out onto a lightly floured surface and knead for about 8-10 minutes, or until it becomes smooth and elastic. The dough should be soft but not too sticky.
6. **First Rise:**
    - Place the dough in a lightly greased bowl and cover it with plastic wrap or a damp cloth. Let it rise in a warm place for about 1-1.5 hours, or until it has doubled in size.
7. **Shape the Loaf:**

- Punch down the risen dough and turn it out onto a floured surface. Shape the dough into a loaf by flattening it slightly and rolling it up tightly from one edge to the other.
- Place the shaped loaf into a greased 9x5 inch (23x13 cm) loaf pan.

8. **Second Rise:**
   - Cover the loaf with plastic wrap or a damp cloth and let it rise for another 30-45 minutes, or until it has risen noticeably.
9. **Preheat Oven:**
   - Preheat your oven to 375°F (190°C).
10. **Prepare for Baking:**
    - If desired, sprinkle the top of the loaf with rolled oats or wheat bran for added texture and visual appeal.
11. **Bake:**
    - Bake in the preheated oven for 30-35 minutes, or until the bread is golden brown and sounds hollow when tapped on the bottom.
12. **Cool:**
    - Allow the bread to cool in the pan for about 10 minutes before transferring it to a wire rack to cool completely.

Notes:

- **Texture:** Whole wheat flour gives the bread a denser texture and a richer flavor compared to white bread. It's also higher in fiber and nutrients.
- **Flour:** Adjust the amount of all-purpose flour if the dough seems too sticky. Whole wheat flour can vary in absorbency.
- **Sweetener:** Honey can be used in place of granulated sugar for a more natural sweetener.

Enjoy your Canadian Wheat Bread fresh out of the oven or toasted with your favorite spreads! It's a nutritious and tasty option for any meal.

Lemon Blueberry Scones

Ingredients:

- **For the Scones:**
    - 2 cups (250 g) all-purpose flour
    - 1/4 cup (50 g) granulated sugar
    - 1 tablespoon (15 g) baking powder
    - 1/2 teaspoon (2.5 g) salt
    - 1/2 cup (115 g) cold unsalted butter, cut into small pieces
    - 1 cup (150 g) fresh or frozen blueberries (if using frozen, do not thaw)
    - 1 tablespoon (15 ml) lemon zest (from about 1 lemon)
    - 1 large egg
    - 1/2 cup (120 ml) heavy cream
    - 1 teaspoon (5 ml) vanilla extract
- **For the Lemon Glaze (optional):**
    - 1 cup (120 g) powdered sugar
    - 2 tablespoons (30 ml) fresh lemon juice
    - 1 teaspoon (5 ml) lemon zest

Instructions:

1. **Preheat Oven:**
    - Preheat your oven to 400°F (200°C). Line a baking sheet with parchment paper or a silicone baking mat.
2. **Mix Dry Ingredients:**
    - In a large mixing bowl, whisk together the flour, granulated sugar, baking powder, and salt.
3. **Cut in the Butter:**
    - Add the cold, cubed butter to the dry ingredients. Using a pastry cutter, fork, or your fingers, cut the butter into the flour mixture until it resembles coarse crumbs with pea-sized pieces of butter remaining.
4. **Add Blueberries and Lemon Zest:**
    - Gently fold in the blueberries and lemon zest, being careful not to crush the blueberries.
5. **Combine Wet Ingredients:**
    - In a separate bowl, whisk together the egg, heavy cream, and vanilla extract.
6. **Mix the Dough:**
    - Pour the wet ingredients into the dry ingredients and stir until just combined. The dough will be somewhat sticky. Be careful not to overmix, as this can lead to tough scones.
7. **Shape the Scones:**

- Turn the dough out onto a lightly floured surface and gently knead it a few times until it comes together. Pat the dough into a 1-inch (2.5 cm) thick circle.
- Use a sharp knife or a dough cutter to cut the dough into 8 wedges. Alternatively, you can use a round cutter to cut out individual scones.

8. **Prepare for Baking:**
   - Place the scone wedges or rounds onto the prepared baking sheet. If desired, brush the tops with a little extra cream or milk and sprinkle with a bit of sugar for added sweetness and crunch.

9. **Bake:**
   - Bake in the preheated oven for 15-20 minutes, or until the scones are golden brown on top and cooked through.

10. **Cool:**
    - Allow the scones to cool slightly on a wire rack before glazing.

11. **Prepare the Lemon Glaze (optional):**
    - While the scones are cooling, whisk together the powdered sugar, fresh lemon juice, and lemon zest until smooth. If the glaze is too thick, add a bit more lemon juice. If too thin, add a little more powdered sugar.

12. **Glaze the Scones (optional):**
    - Drizzle the lemon glaze over the slightly cooled scones.

Notes:

- **Blueberries:** If using frozen blueberries, keep them frozen until mixing to prevent them from bleeding into the dough.
- **Lemon Zest:** Fresh lemon zest adds vibrant flavor. Be sure to use a microplane or fine grater to zest the lemon.
- **Texture:** The key to flaky scones is to handle the dough as little as possible and to use cold butter.

Enjoy your Lemon Blueberry Scones fresh out of the oven or at room temperature. They pair beautifully with tea or coffee and make a delightful addition to any meal!

Maple Pecan Loaf

Ingredients:

- **For the Loaf:**
    - 1 cup (240 ml) pure maple syrup
    - 1/2 cup (115 g) unsalted butter, softened
    - 1/2 cup (100 g) granulated sugar
    - 2 large eggs
    - 1 teaspoon (5 ml) vanilla extract
    - 2 cups (250 g) all-purpose flour
    - 1 tablespoon (15 g) baking powder
    - 1/2 teaspoon (2.5 g) salt
    - 1/2 cup (120 ml) milk
    - 1 cup (120 g) chopped pecans (lightly toasted, if desired)
- **For the Maple Glaze (optional):**
    - 1/2 cup (60 g) powdered sugar
    - 2-3 tablespoons (30-45 ml) pure maple syrup
    - 1/2 teaspoon (2.5 ml) vanilla extract

Instructions:

1. **Preheat Oven:**
    - Preheat your oven to 350°F (175°C). Grease and flour a 9x5 inch (23x13 cm) loaf pan or line it with parchment paper.
2. **Cream Butter and Sugar:**
    - In a large mixing bowl, cream together the softened butter and granulated sugar until light and fluffy.
3. **Add Maple Syrup and Eggs:**
    - Beat in the maple syrup, eggs, and vanilla extract until well combined.
4. **Mix Dry Ingredients:**
    - In a separate bowl, whisk together the flour, baking powder, and salt.
5. **Combine Wet and Dry Ingredients:**
    - Gradually add the dry ingredients to the wet mixture, alternating with the milk, beginning and ending with the dry ingredients. Stir until just combined. Be careful not to overmix.
6. **Fold in Pecans:**
    - Gently fold in the chopped pecans.
7. **Pour into Pan:**
    - Pour the batter into the prepared loaf pan and smooth the top with a spatula.
8. **Bake:**
    - Bake in the preheated oven for 50-60 minutes, or until a toothpick inserted into the center comes out clean and the top is golden brown.

9. **Cool:**
   - Allow the loaf to cool in the pan for about 10 minutes before transferring it to a wire rack to cool completely.
10. **Prepare the Maple Glaze (optional):**
    - In a small bowl, whisk together the powdered sugar, maple syrup, and vanilla extract until smooth. Adjust the consistency by adding more maple syrup or powdered sugar as needed.
11. **Glaze the Loaf (optional):**
    - Drizzle the maple glaze over the cooled loaf.

Notes:

- **Pecans:** Toasting the pecans lightly before adding them enhances their flavor and crunch. To toast, place them in a dry skillet over medium heat, stirring frequently, until fragrant and slightly darker.
- **Maple Syrup:** Use pure maple syrup for the best flavor. Avoid imitation syrup, which can affect the taste.
- **Storage:** Store the loaf in an airtight container at room temperature for up to 3 days. It can also be wrapped tightly and frozen for up to 3 months.

Enjoy your Maple Pecan Loaf with a cup of tea or coffee, or simply on its own. It's a deliciously sweet and nutty treat that's sure to be a hit!

Saskatoon Berry Bread

Ingredients:

- **For the Bread:**
    - 2 cups (250 g) all-purpose flour
    - 1 cup (120 g) whole wheat flour
    - 1/2 cup (100 g) granulated sugar
    - 2 teaspoons (10 g) baking powder
    - 1/2 teaspoon (2.5 g) salt
    - 1/2 cup (115 g) unsalted butter, softened
    - 1 cup (240 ml) milk
    - 2 large eggs
    - 1 teaspoon (5 ml) vanilla extract
    - 1 1/2 cups (200 g) fresh or frozen Saskatoon berries (if using frozen, do not thaw)
    - 1 tablespoon (15 g) all-purpose flour (for coating berries)
- **For the Topping (optional):**
    - 2 tablespoons (25 g) granulated sugar
    - 1 teaspoon (5 ml) ground cinnamon

Instructions:

1. **Preheat Oven:**
    - Preheat your oven to 350°F (175°C). Grease and flour a 9x5 inch (23x13 cm) loaf pan or line it with parchment paper.
2. **Mix Dry Ingredients:**
    - In a large bowl, whisk together the all-purpose flour, whole wheat flour, granulated sugar, baking powder, and salt.
3. **Prepare the Butter Mixture:**
    - In another bowl, cream together the softened butter and remaining sugar until light and fluffy.
4. **Combine Wet Ingredients:**
    - Beat in the eggs, one at a time, then add the vanilla extract. Mix well.
5. **Combine Dry and Wet Ingredients:**
    - Gradually add the dry ingredients to the wet ingredients, alternating with the milk. Begin and end with the dry ingredients. Mix until just combined. Be careful not to overmix.
6. **Prepare the Saskatoon Berries:**
    - Toss the Saskatoon berries with 1 tablespoon of flour to coat them. This helps to prevent the berries from sinking to the bottom of the loaf.
7. **Fold in the Berries:**
    - Gently fold the coated berries into the batter.
8. **Pour into Pan:**

- Pour the batter into the prepared loaf pan and smooth the top with a spatula.
9. **Prepare for Topping (optional):**
    - In a small bowl, mix the granulated sugar and ground cinnamon. Sprinkle this mixture evenly over the top of the batter.
10. **Bake:**
    - Bake in the preheated oven for 55-65 minutes, or until a toothpick inserted into the center comes out clean and the top is golden brown.
11. **Cool:**
    - Allow the bread to cool in the pan for about 10 minutes before transferring it to a wire rack to cool completely.

Notes:

- **Saskatoon Berries:** If using frozen berries, do not thaw them before adding to the batter to prevent excess moisture.
- **Texture:** The flour coating helps the berries distribute evenly throughout the bread and prevents them from sinking.
- **Storage:** Store the cooled bread in an airtight container at room temperature for up to 3 days. It can also be wrapped tightly and frozen for up to 3 months.

Enjoy your Saskatoon Berry Bread with a pat of butter or a dollop of cream cheese. It's a wonderful way to showcase the unique flavor of Saskatoon berries!

Wild Rice Bread

Ingredients:

- **For the Wild Rice:**
    - 1 cup (200 g) wild rice
    - 2 ½ cups (600 ml) water or vegetable broth
- **For the Bread:**
    - 2 cups (250 g) all-purpose flour
    - 1 cup (125 g) whole wheat flour
    - 1/4 cup (50 g) granulated sugar
    - 2 teaspoons (10 g) baking powder
    - 1 teaspoon (5 g) salt
    - 1 cup (240 ml) buttermilk or milk
    - 1/2 cup (115 g) unsalted butter, melted
    - 2 large eggs
    - 1 teaspoon (5 ml) vanilla extract (optional)
    - 1 cup (150 g) cooked wild rice (cooled)
    - 1/2 cup (50 g) chopped nuts or seeds (optional, for added texture)

Instructions:

1. **Cook the Wild Rice:**
    - Rinse the wild rice under cold water. In a medium saucepan, combine the wild rice and water or vegetable broth. Bring to a boil, then reduce the heat to low, cover, and simmer for 45-60 minutes, or until the rice is tender and the grains have burst open.
    - Drain any excess liquid and let the rice cool to room temperature.
2. **Preheat Oven:**
    - Preheat your oven to 350°F (175°C). Grease and flour a 9x5 inch (23x13 cm) loaf pan or line it with parchment paper.
3. **Mix Dry Ingredients:**
    - In a large mixing bowl, whisk together the all-purpose flour, whole wheat flour, granulated sugar, baking powder, and salt.
4. **Combine Wet Ingredients:**
    - In a separate bowl, whisk together the buttermilk (or milk), melted butter, eggs, and vanilla extract (if using).
5. **Combine Dry and Wet Ingredients:**
    - Gradually add the wet ingredients to the dry ingredients, stirring until just combined. Do not overmix.
6. **Add Wild Rice:**
    - Fold the cooled wild rice into the batter. If you're adding nuts or seeds, fold them in as well.
7. **Pour into Pan:**
    - Pour the batter into the prepared loaf pan and smooth the top with a spatula.

8. **Bake:**
   - Bake in the preheated oven for 50-60 minutes, or until a toothpick inserted into the center comes out clean and the top is golden brown.
9. **Cool:**
   - Allow the bread to cool in the pan for about 10 minutes before transferring it to a wire rack to cool completely.

Notes:

- **Wild Rice:** Ensure that the wild rice is fully cooked and cooled before adding it to the batter to avoid affecting the texture of the bread.
- **Texture:** Wild rice adds a unique texture to the bread, making it hearty and slightly chewy.
- **Storage:** Store the cooled bread in an airtight container at room temperature for up to 3 days. It can also be wrapped tightly and frozen for up to 3 months.

Enjoy your Wild Rice Bread fresh out of the oven or toasted with your favorite spread. It's a wholesome and distinctive bread that pairs wonderfully with a variety of dishes.

Canadian Cheddar Chive Bread

Ingredients:

- **For the Bread:**
    - 2 cups (250 g) all-purpose flour
    - 1 cup (120 g) whole wheat flour
    - 1 tablespoon (15 g) granulated sugar
    - 1 tablespoon (15 g) baking powder
    - 1 teaspoon (5 g) salt
    - 1 cup (115 g) shredded sharp Canadian cheddar cheese
    - 1/4 cup (60 ml) finely chopped fresh chives
    - 1 cup (240 ml) milk
    - 1/2 cup (115 g) unsalted butter, melted
    - 2 large eggs

Instructions:

1. **Preheat Oven:**
    - Preheat your oven to 350°F (175°C). Grease and flour a 9x5 inch (23x13 cm) loaf pan or line it with parchment paper.
2. **Mix Dry Ingredients:**
    - In a large mixing bowl, whisk together the all-purpose flour, whole wheat flour, granulated sugar, baking powder, and salt.
3. **Add Cheese and Chives:**
    - Stir in the shredded cheddar cheese and chopped chives until well distributed throughout the dry ingredients.
4. **Combine Wet Ingredients:**
    - In a separate bowl, whisk together the milk, melted butter, and eggs until well combined.
5. **Combine Dry and Wet Ingredients:**
    - Pour the wet ingredients into the dry ingredients and stir until just combined. Be careful not to overmix.
6. **Pour into Pan:**
    - Pour the batter into the prepared loaf pan and smooth the top with a spatula.
7. **Bake:**
    - Bake in the preheated oven for 45-55 minutes, or until a toothpick inserted into the center comes out clean and the top is golden brown.
8. **Cool:**
    - Allow the bread to cool in the pan for about 10 minutes before transferring it to a wire rack to cool completely.

Notes:

- **Cheese:** Sharp Canadian cheddar adds a robust flavor to the bread. Feel free to use medium or mild cheddar if you prefer a less intense cheese flavor.
- **Chives:** Fresh chives give the bread a mild onion flavor. You can adjust the amount to taste.
- **Texture:** This bread is best served warm or toasted. It has a soft, slightly crumbly texture due to the cheese.

Storage: Store the cooled bread in an airtight container at room temperature for up to 3 days. It can also be wrapped tightly and frozen for up to 3 months. Reheat in the oven or toast slices to refresh.

Enjoy your Canadian Cheddar Chive Bread with a hearty soup, a fresh salad, or simply on its own. Its cheesy, herb-infused flavor makes it a versatile and satisfying choice.

Buttermilk Cornbread

Ingredients:

- **For the Cornbread:**
    - 1 cup (120 g) cornmeal
    - 1 cup (125 g) all-purpose flour
    - 1/4 cup (50 g) granulated sugar
    - 1 tablespoon (15 g) baking powder
    - 1/2 teaspoon (2.5 g) baking soda
    - 1/2 teaspoon (2.5 g) salt
    - 1 cup (240 ml) buttermilk
    - 1/2 cup (115 g) unsalted butter, melted
    - 2 large eggs
- **For the Pan (optional but recommended):**
    - 2 tablespoons (30 g) unsalted butter

Instructions:

1. **Preheat Oven:**
    - Preheat your oven to 400°F (200°C). Place a 9-inch (23 cm) cast-iron skillet or baking dish in the oven to heat.
2. **Mix Dry Ingredients:**
    - In a large mixing bowl, whisk together the cornmeal, all-purpose flour, granulated sugar, baking powder, baking soda, and salt.
3. **Combine Wet Ingredients:**
    - In another bowl, whisk together the buttermilk, melted butter, and eggs until well combined.
4. **Combine Dry and Wet Ingredients:**
    - Pour the wet ingredients into the dry ingredients and stir until just combined. The batter will be lumpy, but that's okay—don't overmix.
5. **Prepare the Pan:**
    - Carefully remove the preheated skillet or baking dish from the oven. If using, add the 2 tablespoons of butter to the hot pan and swirl it around to coat the bottom and sides.
6. **Pour Batter into Pan:**
    - Pour the cornbread batter into the hot, buttered skillet or baking dish. The batter should sizzle as it hits the hot pan.
7. **Bake:**
    - Bake in the preheated oven for 20-25 minutes, or until the top is golden brown and a toothpick inserted into the center comes out clean.
8. **Cool:**

- Allow the cornbread to cool in the pan for about 10 minutes before slicing and serving.

Notes:

- **Cast-Iron Skillet:** Using a cast-iron skillet helps create a crispy crust on the cornbread. If you don't have one, you can use any oven-safe baking dish.
- **Texture:** This cornbread is slightly sweet and very moist due to the buttermilk. The edges should be crispy while the interior remains tender.
- **Add-Ins:** Feel free to mix in ingredients like corn kernels, shredded cheese, or chopped jalapeños for added flavor.

Storage: Store leftover cornbread in an airtight container at room temperature for up to 3 days. For longer storage, wrap it tightly and freeze for up to 3 months. Reheat in the oven or toaster for best results.

Enjoy your Buttermilk Cornbread warm, with a pat of butter, or alongside your favorite hearty dishes!

Timothy Hay Bread

Ingredients:

- **For the Bread:**
    - 1 cup (240 ml) hot water
    - 1/2 cup (120 ml) timothy hay tea (made from steeping 1/4 cup of dried timothy hay in hot water for 10 minutes, then straining)
    - 1 tablespoon (15 g) granulated sugar
    - 1 tablespoon (9 g) active dry yeast
    - 3 cups (375 g) all-purpose flour
    - 1 cup (125 g) whole wheat flour
    - 1 teaspoon (5 g) salt
    - 1/4 cup (60 ml) olive oil or melted butter
    - 1 large egg (optional, for added richness)
- **For the Topping (optional):**
    - 1 tablespoon (15 ml) olive oil
    - 1 tablespoon (10 g) sesame seeds or sunflower seeds

Instructions:

1. **Prepare the Timothy Hay Tea:**
    - In a small pot, bring 1 cup of water to a boil. Add 1/4 cup dried timothy hay and steep for about 10 minutes. Strain and set the tea aside to cool slightly.
2. **Activate the Yeast:**
    - In a large mixing bowl, combine the hot water, timothy hay tea, and granulated sugar. Sprinkle the active dry yeast over the mixture and let it sit for about 5-10 minutes, or until the yeast is frothy.
3. **Mix Dry Ingredients:**
    - In another bowl, whisk together the all-purpose flour, whole wheat flour, and salt.
4. **Combine Ingredients:**
    - Add the flour mixture to the yeast mixture, followed by the olive oil (or melted butter) and the egg (if using). Mix until a dough forms.
5. **Knead the Dough:**
    - Turn the dough out onto a lightly floured surface and knead for about 8-10 minutes, or until smooth and elastic. Add more flour as needed if the dough is too sticky.
6. **Let the Dough Rise:**
    - Place the dough in a lightly oiled bowl, cover it with a damp cloth or plastic wrap, and let it rise in a warm place for about 1-1.5 hours, or until doubled in size.
7. **Shape and Second Rise:**

- Punch down the dough and shape it into a loaf. Place it in a greased 9x5 inch (23x13 cm) loaf pan. Cover and let it rise again for about 30-45 minutes, or until it has risen slightly above the edge of the pan.

8. **Preheat Oven:**
   - Preheat your oven to 375°F (190°C).
9. **Prepare for Baking:**
   - Brush the top of the loaf with olive oil and sprinkle with sesame seeds or sunflower seeds, if desired.
10. **Bake:**
    - Bake in the preheated oven for 30-35 minutes, or until the bread is golden brown and sounds hollow when tapped on the bottom.
11. **Cool:**
    - Allow the bread to cool in the pan for about 10 minutes before transferring it to a wire rack to cool completely.

Notes:

- **Timothy Hay:** Timothy hay used in this recipe should be free of chemicals and additives. It's essential to ensure that it's safe for consumption.
- **Flavor Profile:** The bread has a mild, earthy flavor due to the timothy hay tea. It pairs well with savory dishes and can be enjoyed toasted with butter or cheese.
- **Texture:** This bread is slightly denser than typical white bread but still soft and flavorful.

Storage: Store the cooled bread in an airtight container at room temperature for up to 3 days. For longer storage, wrap it tightly and freeze for up to 3 months.

Enjoy your Timothy Hay Bread as a unique and wholesome addition to your bread repertoire!

Nova Scotia Brown Bread

Ingredients:

- **For the Bread:**
    - 2 cups (250 g) whole wheat flour
    - 1 cup (125 g) all-purpose flour
    - 1/4 cup (50 g) granulated sugar or brown sugar
    - 1 tablespoon (15 g) baking powder
    - 1 teaspoon (5 g) salt
    - 1 cup (240 ml) buttermilk or milk
    - 1/4 cup (60 ml) molasses
    - 1/4 cup (60 g) unsalted butter, melted
    - 2 large eggs
- **For the Topping (optional):**
    - 1 tablespoon (15 ml) melted butter
    - 1 tablespoon (10 g) rolled oats or sesame seeds

Instructions:

1. **Preheat Oven:**
    - Preheat your oven to 350°F (175°C). Grease and flour a 9x5 inch (23x13 cm) loaf pan or line it with parchment paper.
2. **Mix Dry Ingredients:**
    - In a large mixing bowl, whisk together the whole wheat flour, all-purpose flour, sugar (or brown sugar), baking powder, and salt.
3. **Combine Wet Ingredients:**
    - In a separate bowl, whisk together the buttermilk (or milk), molasses, melted butter, and eggs until well combined.
4. **Combine Dry and Wet Ingredients:**
    - Pour the wet ingredients into the dry ingredients and stir until just combined. The batter will be thick and slightly lumpy.
5. **Pour into Pan:**
    - Pour the batter into the prepared loaf pan and smooth the top with a spatula.
6. **Prepare for Topping (optional):**
    - Brush the top of the loaf with melted butter and sprinkle with rolled oats or sesame seeds, if desired.
7. **Bake:**
    - Bake in the preheated oven for 50-60 minutes, or until a toothpick inserted into the center comes out clean and the top is golden brown.
8. **Cool:**
    - Allow the bread to cool in the pan for about 10 minutes before transferring it to a wire rack to cool completely.

Notes:

- **Molasses:** Adds a rich, slightly sweet flavor and helps to create a moist texture. You can adjust the amount to taste or substitute with honey or brown sugar if preferred.
- **Texture:** This bread is denser than white bread and has a hearty texture due to the whole wheat flour. It's ideal for slicing and serving with butter or cheese.
- **Storage:** Store the cooled bread in an airtight container at room temperature for up to 3 days. For longer storage, wrap it tightly and freeze for up to 3 months. Reheat slices in the toaster or oven to refresh.

Enjoy your Nova Scotia Brown Bread with a hearty stew, a slice of cheese, or just as is for a satisfying, wholesome treat!

Montreal Rye with Caraway Seeds

Ingredients:

- **For the Rye Dough:**
    - 1 1/2 cups (360 ml) warm water (110°F/45°C)
    - 1 tablespoon (15 g) granulated sugar
    - 2 teaspoons (6 g) active dry yeast
    - 2 cups (250 g) rye flour
    - 1 1/2 cups (190 g) all-purpose flour
    - 1 tablespoon (10 g) caraway seeds
    - 1 tablespoon (15 g) kosher salt
    - 2 tablespoons (30 ml) vegetable oil or melted butter
    - 1/4 cup (60 ml) molasses or honey
    - 1/2 teaspoon (2.5 g) ground black pepper (optional)
- **For the Topping (optional):**
    - 1 tablespoon (10 g) caraway seeds
    - 1 tablespoon (15 ml) water

Instructions:

1. **Activate the Yeast:**
    - In a small bowl, combine the warm water and granulated sugar. Sprinkle the yeast over the mixture and let it sit for 5-10 minutes, or until frothy.
2. **Mix Dry Ingredients:**
    - In a large mixing bowl, whisk together the rye flour, all-purpose flour, caraway seeds, and salt.
3. **Combine Wet Ingredients:**
    - Add the molasses (or honey), vegetable oil (or melted butter), and ground black pepper (if using) to the yeast mixture. Stir to combine.
4. **Combine Dry and Wet Ingredients:**
    - Pour the wet ingredients into the dry ingredients and mix until a dough forms. The dough will be sticky but manageable.
5. **Knead the Dough:**
    - Turn the dough out onto a lightly floured surface and knead for about 8-10 minutes, or until smooth and elastic. Add more all-purpose flour as needed if the dough is too sticky.
6. **First Rise:**
    - Place the dough in a lightly oiled bowl, cover it with a damp cloth or plastic wrap, and let it rise in a warm place for 1-1.5 hours, or until doubled in size.
7. **Shape the Dough:**
    - Punch down the dough and turn it out onto a lightly floured surface. Shape it into a loaf and place it in a greased 9x5 inch (23x13 cm) loaf pan. Alternatively, you can shape it into a round loaf and place it on a parchment-lined baking sheet.
8. **Prepare for Second Rise:**

- Cover the shaped dough and let it rise again for 30-45 minutes, or until it has risen slightly above the edge of the pan or has doubled in size if shaped as a round loaf.

9. **Preheat Oven:**
   - Preheat your oven to 375°F (190°C).
10. **Prepare for Baking:**
    - For a decorative touch, brush the top of the loaf with water and sprinkle with additional caraway seeds.
11. **Bake:**
    - Bake in the preheated oven for 35-45 minutes, or until the bread is dark brown and sounds hollow when tapped on the bottom. The internal temperature should be about 190°F (88°C).
12. **Cool:**
    - Allow the bread to cool in the pan for 10 minutes before transferring it to a wire rack to cool completely.

Notes:

- **Rye Flour:** Rye flour gives the bread its characteristic flavor and density. Mixing with all-purpose flour helps improve the texture and rise.
- **Caraway Seeds:** Essential for the traditional flavor of Montreal Rye Bread, but you can adjust the amount to taste.
- **Texture:** This bread has a dense, hearty texture and a slightly tangy flavor from the rye. It pairs well with sandwiches, soups, or simply with butter.

Storage: Store the cooled bread in an airtight container at room temperature for up to 3 days. For longer storage, wrap it tightly and freeze for up to 3 months. Reheat slices in the toaster or oven to refresh.

Enjoy your Montreal Rye with Caraway Seeds as a satisfying, flavorful addition to any meal!

Cinnamon Raisin Swirl Bread

Ingredients:

- **For the Dough:**
    - 1 cup (240 ml) warm milk (110°F/45°C)
    - 1/4 cup (50 g) granulated sugar
    - 2 1/4 teaspoons (7 g) active dry yeast
    - 1/4 cup (60 g) unsalted butter, softened
    - 1 large egg
    - 3 1/2 cups (440 g) all-purpose flour
    - 1/2 teaspoon (2.5 g) salt
- **For the Cinnamon Swirl:**
    - 1/2 cup (100 g) granulated sugar
    - 2 tablespoons (15 g) ground cinnamon
    - 1/4 cup (60 g) unsalted butter, melted
    - 1 cup (150 g) raisins
- **For the Egg Wash (optional):**
    - 1 large egg, beaten
    - 1 tablespoon (15 ml) water

Instructions:

1. **Activate the Yeast:**
    - In a small bowl, combine the warm milk and granulated sugar. Sprinkle the yeast over the mixture and let it sit for about 5-10 minutes, or until frothy.
2. **Mix Dough Ingredients:**
    - In a large mixing bowl, combine the yeast mixture with the softened butter and egg. Stir to combine.
    - Gradually add the all-purpose flour and salt, mixing until a dough forms.
3. **Knead the Dough:**
    - Turn the dough out onto a lightly floured surface and knead for about 8-10 minutes, or until the dough is smooth and elastic. Add more flour if needed if the dough is too sticky.
4. **First Rise:**
    - Place the dough in a lightly oiled bowl, cover it with a damp cloth or plastic wrap, and let it rise in a warm place for 1-1.5 hours, or until doubled in size.
5. **Prepare Cinnamon Filling:**
    - In a small bowl, mix together the granulated sugar and ground cinnamon. Set aside.
6. **Shape the Bread:**
    - Punch down the dough and turn it out onto a lightly floured surface. Roll the dough into a large rectangle, about 12x18 inches (30x45 cm).

- Brush the melted butter evenly over the dough. Sprinkle the cinnamon sugar mixture evenly over the butter. Scatter the raisins over the cinnamon sugar.
7. **Form the Swirl:**
    - Starting from one long side, carefully roll the dough up tightly into a log. Pinch the seams to seal.
8. **Place in Pan:**
    - Grease a 9x5 inch (23x13 cm) loaf pan. Place the rolled dough seam-side down in the pan, tucking the ends underneath.
9. **Second Rise:**
    - Cover the loaf pan with a damp cloth or plastic wrap and let the dough rise again for about 30-45 minutes, or until it has risen slightly above the edge of the pan.
10. **Preheat Oven:**
    - Preheat your oven to 350°F (175°C).
11. **Apply Egg Wash (Optional):**
    - Brush the top of the loaf with the beaten egg mixed with water for a glossy finish.
12. **Bake:**
    - Bake in the preheated oven for 35-40 minutes, or until the bread is golden brown and sounds hollow when tapped on the bottom.
13. **Cool:**
    - Allow the bread to cool in the pan for about 10 minutes before transferring it to a wire rack to cool completely.

Notes:

- **Texture:** This bread has a soft and slightly sweet texture with a delightful cinnamon swirl. It's best enjoyed fresh or toasted.
- **Raisins:** Soaking the raisins in a bit of hot water before adding them can help plump them up and keep them moist in the bread.
- **Variations:** For a nutty twist, you can add chopped nuts to the cinnamon sugar mixture.

Storage: Store the cooled bread in an airtight container at room temperature for up to 3 days. For longer storage, wrap it tightly and freeze for up to 3 months. Reheat slices in the toaster or oven to refresh.

Enjoy your homemade Cinnamon Raisin Swirl Bread as a warm, comforting treat with a cup of coffee or tea!

Canadian Honey Whole Wheat Bread

Ingredients:

- **For the Dough:**
    - 1 1/2 cups (360 ml) warm water (110°F/45°C)
    - 1/4 cup (60 ml) honey
    - 2 1/4 teaspoons (7 g) active dry yeast
    - 1/4 cup (60 ml) vegetable oil or melted butter
    - 2 cups (250 g) whole wheat flour
    - 1 1/2 cups (190 g) all-purpose flour
    - 1 teaspoon (5 g) salt
- **For the Topping (optional):**
    - 1 tablespoon (15 ml) milk or water
    - 1 tablespoon (10 g) rolled oats or sunflower seeds

Instructions:

1. **Activate the Yeast:**
    - In a small bowl, combine the warm water and honey. Sprinkle the yeast over the mixture and let it sit for about 5-10 minutes, or until frothy.
2. **Mix Dough Ingredients:**
    - In a large mixing bowl, combine the yeast mixture with the vegetable oil (or melted butter). Stir to combine.
    - Gradually add the whole wheat flour and salt, mixing until combined.
3. **Add All-Purpose Flour:**
    - Add the all-purpose flour a little at a time, mixing until the dough starts to come together. Continue adding flour until the dough is slightly sticky but manageable.
4. **Knead the Dough:**
    - Turn the dough out onto a lightly floured surface and knead for about 8-10 minutes, or until smooth and elastic. The dough should be soft but not too sticky.
5. **First Rise:**
    - Place the dough in a lightly oiled bowl, cover it with a damp cloth or plastic wrap, and let it rise in a warm place for 1-1.5 hours, or until doubled in size.
6. **Shape the Bread:**
    - Punch down the dough and turn it out onto a lightly floured surface. Shape it into a loaf and place it in a greased 9x5 inch (23x13 cm) loaf pan.
7. **Prepare for Second Rise:**
    - Cover the pan with a damp cloth or plastic wrap and let the dough rise again for about 30-45 minutes, or until it has risen slightly above the edge of the pan.
8. **Preheat Oven:**
    - Preheat your oven to 350°F (175°C).
9. **Prepare for Baking:**

- Brush the top of the loaf with milk or water and sprinkle with rolled oats or sunflower seeds if desired.

10. **Bake:**
    - Bake in the preheated oven for 35-40 minutes, or until the bread is golden brown and sounds hollow when tapped on the bottom. The internal temperature should be about 190°F (88°C).
11. **Cool:**
    - Allow the bread to cool in the pan for about 10 minutes before transferring it to a wire rack to cool completely.

Notes:

- **Honey:** Adds natural sweetness and moisture to the bread. If you prefer a less sweet bread, you can adjust the amount of honey to taste.
- **Whole Wheat Flour:** Gives the bread a denser texture and a nutty flavor. Mixing with all-purpose flour helps to lighten the texture.
- **Texture:** This bread has a hearty, satisfying texture with a slightly sweet flavor. It's perfect for hearty sandwiches or toasted with a bit of butter.

Storage: Store the cooled bread in an airtight container at room temperature for up to 3 days. For longer storage, wrap it tightly and freeze for up to 3 months. Reheat slices in the toaster or oven to refresh.

Enjoy your Canadian Honey Whole Wheat Bread fresh out of the oven or as part of a delicious meal!

Maple Raisin Bread

Ingredients:

- **For the Dough:**
    - 1 cup (240 ml) warm milk (110°F/45°C)
    - 1/4 cup (60 ml) pure maple syrup
    - 2 1/4 teaspoons (7 g) active dry yeast
    - 1/4 cup (60 g) unsalted butter, softened
    - 1 large egg
    - 3 cups (375 g) all-purpose flour
    - 1 teaspoon (5 g) salt
    - 1 cup (150 g) raisins
- **For the Topping (optional):**
    - 1 tablespoon (15 ml) milk or water
    - 1 tablespoon (10 g) granulated sugar or coarse sugar

Instructions:

1. **Activate the Yeast:**
    - In a small bowl, combine the warm milk and pure maple syrup. Sprinkle the yeast over the mixture and let it sit for about 5-10 minutes, or until frothy.
2. **Mix Dough Ingredients:**
    - In a large mixing bowl, combine the yeast mixture with the softened butter and egg. Stir to combine.
    - Gradually add the all-purpose flour and salt, mixing until a dough forms.
3. **Add Raisins:**
    - Gently fold in the raisins until evenly distributed in the dough.
4. **Knead the Dough:**
    - Turn the dough out onto a lightly floured surface and knead for about 8-10 minutes, or until smooth and elastic. The dough should be soft but not too sticky.
5. **First Rise:**
    - Place the dough in a lightly oiled bowl, cover it with a damp cloth or plastic wrap, and let it rise in a warm place for 1-1.5 hours, or until doubled in size.
6. **Shape the Bread:**
    - Punch down the dough and turn it out onto a lightly floured surface. Shape it into a loaf and place it in a greased 9x5 inch (23x13 cm) loaf pan.
7. **Prepare for Second Rise:**
    - Cover the pan with a damp cloth or plastic wrap and let the dough rise again for about 30-45 minutes, or until it has risen slightly above the edge of the pan.
8. **Preheat Oven:**
    - Preheat your oven to 350°F (175°C).
9. **Prepare for Baking:**

- Brush the top of the loaf with milk or water and sprinkle with granulated sugar or coarse sugar if desired.

10. **Bake:**
    - Bake in the preheated oven for 35-45 minutes, or until the bread is golden brown and sounds hollow when tapped on the bottom. The internal temperature should be about 190°F (88°C).

11. **Cool:**
    - Allow the bread to cool in the pan for about 10 minutes before transferring it to a wire rack to cool completely.

Notes:

- **Maple Syrup:** Provides natural sweetness and a subtle maple flavor. Use pure maple syrup for the best taste.
- **Raisins:** You can soak the raisins in a bit of warm water for 10 minutes before adding them to the dough to keep them plump and moist.
- **Texture:** This bread is soft with a sweet, slightly chewy texture thanks to the raisins. It's great for sandwiches or toasted with a bit of butter.

Storage: Store the cooled bread in an airtight container at room temperature for up to 3 days. For longer storage, wrap it tightly and freeze for up to 3 months. Reheat slices in the toaster or oven to refresh.

Enjoy your Maple Raisin Bread fresh and warm or toasted with a bit of butter and maybe a drizzle of extra maple syrup!

Spelt and Flaxseed Bread

Ingredients:

- **For the Dough:**
    - 1 cup (240 ml) warm water (110°F/45°C)
    - 2 tablespoons (30 ml) honey or maple syrup
    - 2 1/4 teaspoons (7 g) active dry yeast
    - 1/4 cup (60 ml) olive oil or melted butter
    - 1/4 cup (40 g) ground flaxseeds (flaxmeal)
    - 1 cup (120 g) whole spelt flour
    - 2 cups (250 g) all-purpose flour
    - 1 teaspoon (5 g) salt
- **For the Topping (optional):**
    - 1 tablespoon (15 ml) water
    - 1 tablespoon (10 g) whole flaxseeds

Instructions:

1. **Activate the Yeast:**
    - In a small bowl, combine the warm water and honey (or maple syrup). Sprinkle the yeast over the mixture and let it sit for about 5-10 minutes, or until frothy.
2. **Mix Dough Ingredients:**
    - In a large mixing bowl, combine the yeast mixture with the olive oil (or melted butter) and ground flaxseeds. Stir to combine.
    - Gradually add the spelt flour and salt, mixing until combined.
    - Add the all-purpose flour gradually, mixing until a dough forms.
3. **Knead the Dough:**
    - Turn the dough out onto a lightly floured surface and knead for about 8-10 minutes, or until smooth and elastic. The dough should be soft but not too sticky.
4. **First Rise:**
    - Place the dough in a lightly oiled bowl, cover it with a damp cloth or plastic wrap, and let it rise in a warm place for 1-1.5 hours, or until doubled in size.
5. **Shape the Bread:**
    - Punch down the dough and turn it out onto a lightly floured surface. Shape it into a loaf and place it in a greased 9x5 inch (23x13 cm) loaf pan.
6. **Prepare for Second Rise:**
    - Cover the pan with a damp cloth or plastic wrap and let the dough rise again for about 30-45 minutes, or until it has risen slightly above the edge of the pan.
7. **Preheat Oven:**
    - Preheat your oven to 350°F (175°C).
8. **Prepare for Baking:**
    - Brush the top of the loaf with water and sprinkle with whole flaxseeds if desired.
9. **Bake:**
    - Bake in the preheated oven for 35-45 minutes, or until the bread is golden brown and sounds hollow when tapped on the bottom. The internal temperature should be about 190°F (88°C).

10. **Cool:**
    - Allow the bread to cool in the pan for about 10 minutes before transferring it to a wire rack to cool completely.

Notes:

- **Spelt Flour:** Spelt flour has a nutty flavor and is slightly lighter than whole wheat flour. It can be used in combination with all-purpose flour for a lighter texture.
- **Flaxseeds:** Ground flaxseeds add a nutty flavor and are rich in omega-3 fatty acids. You can also use whole flaxseeds for a bit of added texture and crunch.
- **Texture:** This bread is hearty and has a slightly dense texture due to the spelt flour and flaxseeds. It's great for making sandwiches or enjoying toasted.

Storage: Store the cooled bread in an airtight container at room temperature for up to 3 days. For longer storage, wrap it tightly and freeze for up to 3 months. Reheat slices in the toaster or oven to refresh.

Enjoy your Spelt and Flaxseed Bread fresh out of the oven or as part of a delicious meal!

Prairie Seed Bread

Ingredients:

- **For the Dough:**
    - 1 1/2 cups (360 ml) warm water (110°F/45°C)
    - 1/4 cup (60 ml) honey or maple syrup
    - 2 1/4 teaspoons (7 g) active dry yeast
    - 1/4 cup (60 ml) olive oil or melted butter
    - 1 cup (120 g) whole wheat flour
    - 1 cup (120 g) spelt flour or all-purpose flour
    - 1 1/2 cups (190 g) bread flour
    - 1/4 cup (30 g) sunflower seeds
    - 1/4 cup (30 g) pumpkin seeds
    - 2 tablespoons (20 g) chia seeds
    - 2 tablespoons (20 g) flaxseeds (flaxmeal)
    - 1 teaspoon (5 g) salt
- **For the Topping (optional):**
    - 1 tablespoon (15 ml) water
    - 1 tablespoon (10 g) mixed seeds (sunflower, pumpkin, flaxseeds)

Instructions:

1. **Activate the Yeast:**
    - In a small bowl, combine the warm water and honey (or maple syrup). Sprinkle the yeast over the mixture and let it sit for about 5-10 minutes, or until frothy.
2. **Mix Dough Ingredients:**
    - In a large mixing bowl, combine the yeast mixture with the olive oil (or melted butter). Stir to combine.
    - Add the whole wheat flour, spelt flour (or all-purpose flour), and salt. Mix until combined.
    - Gradually add the bread flour, mixing until a dough forms.
3. **Add Seeds:**
    - Gently fold in the sunflower seeds, pumpkin seeds, chia seeds, and flaxseeds until evenly distributed in the dough.
4. **Knead the Dough:**
    - Turn the dough out onto a lightly floured surface and knead for about 8-10 minutes, or until smooth and elastic. The dough should be soft but not too sticky.
5. **First Rise:**
    - Place the dough in a lightly oiled bowl, cover it with a damp cloth or plastic wrap, and let it rise in a warm place for 1-1.5 hours, or until doubled in size.
6. **Shape the Bread:**

- Punch down the dough and turn it out onto a lightly floured surface. Shape it into a loaf and place it in a greased 9x5 inch (23x13 cm) loaf pan.

7. **Prepare for Second Rise:**
   - Cover the pan with a damp cloth or plastic wrap and let the dough rise again for about 30-45 minutes, or until it has risen slightly above the edge of the pan.
8. **Preheat Oven:**
   - Preheat your oven to 350°F (175°C).
9. **Prepare for Baking:**
   - Brush the top of the loaf with water and sprinkle with mixed seeds if desired for extra texture and a decorative touch.
10. **Bake:**
    - Bake in the preheated oven for 35-45 minutes, or until the bread is golden brown and sounds hollow when tapped on the bottom. The internal temperature should be about 190°F (88°C).
11. **Cool:**
    - Allow the bread to cool in the pan for about 10 minutes before transferring it to a wire rack to cool completely.

Notes:

- **Seed Variations:** You can adjust the types and quantities of seeds based on your preference or what you have on hand.
- **Texture:** This bread is dense and hearty, with a satisfying crunch from the seeds. It's great for sandwiches, as a side with soups, or toasted with a bit of butter.

Storage: Store the cooled bread in an airtight container at room temperature for up to 3 days. For longer storage, wrap it tightly and freeze for up to 3 months. Reheat slices in the toaster or oven to refresh.

Enjoy your Prairie Seed Bread as a nutritious and flavorful addition to your meals!

Canadian Fruit and Nut Bread

Ingredients:

- **For the Dough:**
    - 1 1/2 cups (360 ml) warm milk (110°F/45°C)
    - 1/4 cup (60 ml) pure maple syrup
    - 2 1/4 teaspoons (7 g) active dry yeast
    - 1/4 cup (60 g) unsalted butter, softened
    - 1 large egg
    - 2 cups (250 g) all-purpose flour
    - 1 cup (120 g) whole wheat flour
    - 1 teaspoon (5 g) salt
- **For the Fruit and Nut Mixture:**
    - 1/2 cup (75 g) dried cranberries
    - 1/2 cup (75 g) dried apricots, chopped
    - 1/2 cup (75 g) raisins
    - 1/2 cup (60 g) chopped walnuts or pecans
    - 1/4 cup (30 g) chopped almonds (optional)
- **For the Topping (optional):**
    - 1 tablespoon (15 ml) milk or water
    - 1 tablespoon (10 g) granulated sugar or coarse sugar

Instructions:

1. **Activate the Yeast:**
    - In a small bowl, combine the warm milk and pure maple syrup. Sprinkle the yeast over the mixture and let it sit for about 5-10 minutes, or until frothy.
2. **Mix Dough Ingredients:**
    - In a large mixing bowl, combine the yeast mixture with the softened butter and egg. Stir to combine.
    - Gradually add the all-purpose flour and salt, mixing until combined.
    - Add the whole wheat flour gradually, mixing until a dough forms.
3. **Add Fruit and Nuts:**
    - Gently fold in the dried cranberries, dried apricots, raisins, walnuts (or pecans), and almonds (if using) until evenly distributed in the dough.
4. **Knead the Dough:**
    - Turn the dough out onto a lightly floured surface and knead for about 8-10 minutes, or until smooth and elastic. The dough should be soft but not too sticky.
5. **First Rise:**
    - Place the dough in a lightly oiled bowl, cover it with a damp cloth or plastic wrap, and let it rise in a warm place for 1-1.5 hours, or until doubled in size.
6. **Shape the Bread:**
    - Punch down the dough and turn it out onto a lightly floured surface. Shape it into a loaf and place it in a greased 9x5 inch (23x13 cm) loaf pan.
7. **Prepare for Second Rise:**

- Cover the pan with a damp cloth or plastic wrap and let the dough rise again for about 30-45 minutes, or until it has risen slightly above the edge of the pan.
8. **Preheat Oven:**
    - Preheat your oven to 350°F (175°C).
9. **Prepare for Baking:**
    - Brush the top of the loaf with milk or water and sprinkle with granulated sugar or coarse sugar if desired for a slightly sweet and crunchy topping.
10. **Bake:**
    - Bake in the preheated oven for 35-45 minutes, or until the bread is golden brown and sounds hollow when tapped on the bottom. The internal temperature should be about 190°F (88°C).
11. **Cool:**
    - Allow the bread to cool in the pan for about 10 minutes before transferring it to a wire rack to cool completely.

Notes:

- **Maple Syrup:** Adds a subtle Canadian sweetness to the bread. For a more intense maple flavor, you can increase the amount slightly.
- **Fruit and Nuts:** Feel free to customize the fruit and nut mixture based on your preferences. Other options include dried cherries, figs, or different types of nuts.
- **Texture:** This bread is slightly sweet with a chewy texture from the fruits and a satisfying crunch from the nuts. It's perfect for breakfast or as a snack.

Storage: Store the cooled bread in an airtight container at room temperature for up to 3 days. For longer storage, wrap it tightly and freeze for up to 3 months. Reheat slices in the toaster or oven to refresh.

Enjoy your Canadian Fruit and Nut Bread fresh out of the oven or toasted with a bit of butter or a slice of cheese!

Rosemary Garlic Focaccia

Ingredients:

- **For the Dough:**
    - 1 1/2 cups (360 ml) warm water (110°F/45°C)
    - 2 teaspoons (10 g) sugar
    - 2 1/4 teaspoons (7 g) active dry yeast
    - 1/4 cup (60 ml) olive oil, plus extra for drizzling
    - 4 cups (500 g) all-purpose flour
    - 1 teaspoon (5 g) salt
- **For the Topping:**
    - 2-3 tablespoons (30-45 ml) olive oil
    - 2-3 cloves garlic, thinly sliced
    - 2-3 tablespoons fresh rosemary leaves (or 1-2 tablespoons dried rosemary)
    - 1 teaspoon (5 g) coarse sea salt or kosher salt

Instructions:

1. **Activate the Yeast:**
    - In a small bowl, combine the warm water and sugar. Sprinkle the yeast over the mixture and let it sit for about 5-10 minutes, or until frothy.
2. **Mix Dough Ingredients:**
    - In a large mixing bowl, combine the yeast mixture with 1/4 cup olive oil. Stir to combine.
    - Gradually add the flour and salt, mixing until a dough forms.
3. **Knead the Dough:**
    - Turn the dough out onto a lightly floured surface and knead for about 8-10 minutes, or until smooth and elastic. The dough should be soft but not too sticky.
4. **First Rise:**
    - Place the dough in a lightly oiled bowl, cover it with a damp cloth or plastic wrap, and let it rise in a warm place for 1-1.5 hours, or until doubled in size.
5. **Prepare the Baking Pan:**
    - Preheat your oven to 450°F (230°C). Grease a 13x9 inch (33x23 cm) baking pan with olive oil.
6. **Shape the Dough:**
    - Punch down the dough and turn it out into the prepared baking pan. Use your fingers to spread and press the dough to fit the pan, creating dimples all over the surface.
7. **Prepare for Second Rise:**
    - Cover the pan with a damp cloth or plastic wrap and let the dough rise again for about 20-30 minutes, or until slightly puffed.
8. **Add Toppings:**

- Drizzle the top of the dough with 2-3 tablespoons of olive oil. Scatter the sliced garlic and rosemary leaves evenly over the surface. Sprinkle with coarse sea salt.
9. **Bake:**
    - Bake in the preheated oven for 20-25 minutes, or until the focaccia is golden brown and the edges are crispy.
10. **Cool:**
    - Allow the focaccia to cool in the pan for about 5 minutes before transferring it to a wire rack to cool completely.

Notes:

- **Garlic:** Thinly slice the garlic to ensure it cooks evenly and infuses the bread with flavor.
- **Rosemary:** Fresh rosemary provides a vibrant flavor. If using dried rosemary, crush it slightly to release more flavor.
- **Texture:** Focaccia should be soft and airy on the inside with a crisp crust. The dimples help to create a perfect texture and allow the oil and toppings to infuse the bread.

Storage: Store the cooled focaccia in an airtight container at room temperature for up to 2 days. For longer storage, wrap it tightly and freeze for up to 1 month. Reheat slices in the oven or toaster to refresh.

Enjoy your Rosemary Garlic Focaccia warm from the oven or at room temperature, perhaps with a side of balsamic vinegar and olive oil for dipping!

Dandelion Greens Bread

Ingredients:

- **For the Dough:**
    - 1 cup (240 ml) warm water (110°F/45°C)
    - 2 teaspoons (10 g) sugar
    - 2 1/4 teaspoons (7 g) active dry yeast
    - 1/4 cup (60 ml) olive oil
    - 1/2 cup (120 ml) milk
    - 1 large egg
    - 2 cups (250 g) all-purpose flour
    - 1 cup (120 g) whole wheat flour
    - 1 teaspoon (5 g) salt
- **For the Dandelion Greens Mixture:**
    - 1 cup (60 g) fresh dandelion greens, washed and chopped
    - 2 tablespoons (30 ml) olive oil
    - 1 clove garlic, minced (optional)
    - 1/4 teaspoon (1 g) salt
- **For the Topping (optional):**
    - 1 tablespoon (15 ml) milk or water
    - 1 tablespoon (10 g) coarse sea salt or sesame seeds

Instructions:

1. **Prepare the Dandelion Greens:**
    - In a small skillet, heat 2 tablespoons olive oil over medium heat. Add the chopped dandelion greens and cook for about 3-5 minutes, or until wilted and tender. If using, add the minced garlic during the last minute of cooking. Season with 1/4 teaspoon salt. Allow to cool to room temperature.
2. **Activate the Yeast:**
    - In a small bowl, combine the warm water and sugar. Sprinkle the yeast over the mixture and let it sit for about 5-10 minutes, or until frothy.
3. **Mix Dough Ingredients:**
    - In a large mixing bowl, combine the yeast mixture with the olive oil, milk, and egg. Stir to combine.
    - Gradually add the all-purpose flour and salt, mixing until combined.
    - Add the whole wheat flour gradually, mixing until a dough forms.
4. **Add Dandelion Greens:**
    - Gently fold the cooled dandelion greens mixture into the dough until evenly distributed.
5. **Knead the Dough:**
    - Turn the dough out onto a lightly floured surface and knead for about 8-10 minutes, or until smooth and elastic. The dough should be soft but not too sticky.
6. **First Rise:**
    - Place the dough in a lightly oiled bowl, cover it with a damp cloth or plastic wrap, and let it rise in a warm place for 1-1.5 hours, or until doubled in size.

7. **Shape the Bread:**
   - Punch down the dough and turn it out onto a lightly floured surface. Shape it into a loaf and place it in a greased 9x5 inch (23x13 cm) loaf pan.
8. **Prepare for Second Rise:**
   - Cover the pan with a damp cloth or plastic wrap and let the dough rise again for about 30-45 minutes, or until it has risen slightly above the edge of the pan.
9. **Preheat Oven:**
   - Preheat your oven to 350°F (175°C).
10. **Prepare for Baking:**
    - Brush the top of the loaf with milk or water and sprinkle with coarse sea salt or sesame seeds if desired.
11. **Bake:**
    - Bake in the preheated oven for 35-45 minutes, or until the bread is golden brown and sounds hollow when tapped on the bottom. The internal temperature should be about 190°F (88°C).
12. **Cool:**
    - Allow the bread to cool in the pan for about 10 minutes before transferring it to a wire rack to cool completely.

Notes:

- **Dandelion Greens:** Ensure the dandelion greens are thoroughly washed and chopped before using. Cooking them helps to reduce their bitterness and enhances their flavor.
- **Garlic:** Adding garlic is optional but provides an extra layer of flavor that complements the dandelion greens.
- **Texture:** This bread has a slightly earthy flavor from the dandelion greens and is a great way to incorporate greens into your diet.

Storage: Store the cooled bread in an airtight container at room temperature for up to 3 days. For longer storage, wrap it tightly and freeze for up to 3 months. Reheat slices in the toaster or oven to refresh.

Enjoy your Dandelion Greens Bread as a unique and nutritious addition to your meals!

Vancouver Island Herb Bread

Ingredients:

- **For the Dough:**
    - 1 1/2 cups (360 ml) warm water (110°F/45°C)
    - 2 teaspoons (10 g) sugar
    - 2 1/4 teaspoons (7 g) active dry yeast
    - 1/4 cup (60 ml) olive oil
    - 1 cup (240 ml) buttermilk or milk
    - 1 large egg
    - 4 cups (500 g) all-purpose flour
    - 1 teaspoon (5 g) salt
- **For the Herb Mixture:**
    - 1/4 cup (15 g) fresh parsley, chopped
    - 2 tablespoons (10 g) fresh chives, chopped
    - 1 tablespoon (5 g) fresh thyme leaves
    - 1 tablespoon (5 g) fresh rosemary leaves, chopped
    - 1 clove garlic, minced (optional)
- **For the Topping (optional):**
    - 1 tablespoon (15 ml) olive oil
    - 1 tablespoon (10 g) coarse sea salt or sesame seeds
    - Additional fresh herbs for garnish (optional)

Instructions:

1. **Activate the Yeast:**
    - In a small bowl, combine the warm water and sugar. Sprinkle the yeast over the mixture and let it sit for about 5-10 minutes, or until frothy.
2. **Mix Dough Ingredients:**
    - In a large mixing bowl, combine the yeast mixture with the olive oil, buttermilk (or milk), and egg. Stir to combine.
    - Gradually add the flour and salt, mixing until combined.
3. **Add Herb Mixture:**
    - Fold in the chopped parsley, chives, thyme, rosemary, and minced garlic (if using) until evenly distributed throughout the dough.
4. **Knead the Dough:**
    - Turn the dough out onto a lightly floured surface and knead for about 8-10 minutes, or until smooth and elastic. The dough should be soft but not too sticky.
5. **First Rise:**
    - Place the dough in a lightly oiled bowl, cover it with a damp cloth or plastic wrap, and let it rise in a warm place for 1-1.5 hours, or until doubled in size.
6. **Shape the Bread:**

- Punch down the dough and turn it out onto a lightly floured surface. Shape it into a loaf or divide it into smaller pieces to make rolls, and place them on a greased baking sheet or into greased loaf pans.

7. **Prepare for Second Rise:**
   - Cover the shaped dough with a damp cloth or plastic wrap and let it rise again for about 30-45 minutes, or until it has risen slightly above the edge of the pan or rolls are puffy.

8. **Preheat Oven:**
   - Preheat your oven to 375°F (190°C).

9. **Prepare for Baking:**
   - Brush the top of the loaf or rolls with olive oil and sprinkle with coarse sea salt or sesame seeds if desired. Garnish with additional fresh herbs for extra flavor and a decorative touch.

10. **Bake:**
    - Bake in the preheated oven for 25-35 minutes, or until the bread is golden brown and sounds hollow when tapped on the bottom. The internal temperature should be about 190°F (88°C) for loaves.

11. **Cool:**
    - Allow the bread to cool in the pan for about 10 minutes before transferring it to a wire rack to cool completely.

Notes:

- **Herbs:** Feel free to adjust the herbs based on your preference or what's available. Dried herbs can be used, but fresh herbs will give a more vibrant flavor.
- **Garlic:** Adding garlic provides an additional layer of flavor, but it's optional based on your taste preference.
- **Texture:** This bread will have a slightly crusty exterior and a soft, flavorful interior due to the fresh herbs.

Storage: Store the cooled bread in an airtight container at room temperature for up to 3 days. For longer storage, wrap it tightly and freeze for up to 3 months. Reheat slices in the oven or toaster to refresh.

Enjoy your Vancouver Island Herb Bread as a flavorful accompaniment to any meal or as a delicious standalone treat!

Traditional Bannock with Lard

Ingredients:

- 2 cups (250 g) all-purpose flour
- 1/4 cup (50 g) lard (or unsalted butter if preferred)
- 2 tablespoons (25 g) sugar (optional, for a slightly sweet bannock)
- 1 tablespoon (15 g) baking powder
- 1/2 teaspoon (2.5 g) salt
- 1 cup (240 ml) milk or water
- 1 large egg (optional, for a richer dough)

Instructions:

1. **Prepare the Ingredients:**
   - Preheat your oven to 375°F (190°C) if you're baking the bannock. Alternatively, you can cook it on the stovetop in a skillet or on a griddle.
2. **Mix Dry Ingredients:**
   - In a large mixing bowl, whisk together the flour, baking powder, sugar (if using), and salt.
3. **Incorporate the Lard:**
   - Cut the lard into small pieces and add it to the flour mixture. Using a pastry cutter or your fingers, work the lard into the flour until the mixture resembles coarse crumbs. If using unsalted butter, the process is the same.
4. **Add Wet Ingredients:**
   - Make a well in the center of the flour mixture and pour in the milk (or water) and the egg (if using). Mix until just combined. The dough should be soft but not too sticky. Adjust the liquid or flour as needed.
5. **Shape the Dough:**
   - Turn the dough out onto a lightly floured surface and gently knead it a few times. Pat or roll the dough into a round shape about 1/2 inch (1.3 cm) thick.
6. **Cooking Options:**
   Oven Baking:
   - Place the dough on a baking sheet or in a greased cast-iron skillet. Use a knife to score the top of the dough into wedges or leave it whole.
   - Bake in the preheated oven for 20-25 minutes, or until the top is golden brown and the bread sounds hollow when tapped.
7. **Stovetop Cooking:**
   - Heat a large skillet or griddle over medium heat and lightly grease it with a little oil or lard.
   - Place the dough in the skillet and cook for about 10-15 minutes on each side, or until golden brown and cooked through. Cover the skillet with a lid to help the bread cook evenly if necessary.

8. **Cool:**
    - Allow the bannock to cool slightly before cutting into wedges or slices.

Notes:

- **Lard vs. Butter:** Traditional bannock often uses lard for its authentic flavor and flaky texture. If lard is not available, unsalted butter can be used as a substitute.
- **Sweet vs. Savory:** Adjust the amount of sugar based on your preference. For a savory bannock, you can omit the sugar.
- **Texture:** The texture of bannock can vary based on thickness and cooking method. For a more rustic result, you can shape the dough into a thicker round or oval shape.

Storage: Store any leftover bannock in an airtight container at room temperature for up to 3 days. It can also be frozen for up to 3 months. Reheat in the oven or toaster to refresh.

Enjoy your Traditional Bannock with Lard as a hearty accompaniment to soups, stews, or on its own with a bit of butter or jam!

Honey Oat Loaf

Ingredients:

- **For the Dough:**
    - 1 cup (240 ml) warm water (110°F/45°C)
    - 1/4 cup (60 ml) honey
    - 2 1/4 teaspoons (7 g) active dry yeast
    - 1/4 cup (60 ml) vegetable oil or melted butter
    - 1/2 cup (120 ml) milk
    - 2 cups (250 g) all-purpose flour
    - 1 cup (90 g) rolled oats (not instant)
    - 1 teaspoon (5 g) salt
- **For the Topping (optional):**
    - 1/4 cup (20 g) rolled oats
    - 1 tablespoon (15 ml) honey

Instructions:

1. **Activate the Yeast:**
    - In a small bowl, combine the warm water and honey. Sprinkle the yeast over the mixture and let it sit for about 5-10 minutes, or until frothy.
2. **Mix Dough Ingredients:**
    - In a large mixing bowl, combine the yeast mixture with the oil (or melted butter) and milk. Stir to combine.
    - Gradually add the all-purpose flour, rolled oats, and salt, mixing until a dough forms.
3. **Knead the Dough:**
    - Turn the dough out onto a lightly floured surface and knead for about 8-10 minutes, or until smooth and elastic. The dough should be soft but not too sticky.
4. **First Rise:**
    - Place the dough in a lightly oiled bowl, cover it with a damp cloth or plastic wrap, and let it rise in a warm place for 1-1.5 hours, or until doubled in size.
5. **Shape the Loaf:**
    - Punch down the dough and turn it out onto a lightly floured surface. Shape it into a loaf and place it in a greased 9x5 inch (23x13 cm) loaf pan.
6. **Prepare for Second Rise:**
    - Cover the loaf with a damp cloth or plastic wrap and let it rise again for about 30-45 minutes, or until it has risen slightly above the edge of the pan.
7. **Preheat Oven:**
    - Preheat your oven to 375°F (190°C).
8. **Prepare for Baking:**

- Brush the top of the loaf with a little honey and sprinkle with 1/4 cup of rolled oats for added texture and a nice finish.
9. **Bake:**
    - Bake in the preheated oven for 30-35 minutes, or until the loaf is golden brown and sounds hollow when tapped on the bottom. The internal temperature should be about 190°F (88°C).
10. **Cool:**
    - Allow the loaf to cool in the pan for about 10 minutes before transferring it to a wire rack to cool completely.

Notes:

- **Honey:** Use pure honey for the best flavor. The honey not only sweetens the bread but also contributes to its moistness.
- **Oats:** Rolled oats provide a nice texture and nutty flavor. Avoid instant oats as they can alter the texture of the bread.
- **Texture:** If the dough seems too sticky, add a little more flour. If too dry, add a bit more water or milk.

Storage: Store the cooled bread in an airtight container at room temperature for up to 3 days. It can also be frozen for up to 3 months. To refresh, warm in the oven or toaster.

Enjoy your Honey Oat Loaf as a nutritious and tasty addition to any meal, or simply enjoy a slice with a bit of butter or jam!

Maple Glazed Brioche

Ingredients:

- **For the Brioche Dough:**
    - 1/2 cup (120 ml) whole milk, warmed (110°F/45°C)
    - 1/4 cup (50 g) granulated sugar
    - 2 1/4 teaspoons (7 g) active dry yeast
    - 4 large eggs, at room temperature
    - 1/2 cup (115 g) unsalted butter, softened
    - 3 1/2 cups (440 g) all-purpose flour
    - 1 teaspoon (5 g) salt
- **For the Maple Glaze:**
    - 1/2 cup (120 ml) pure maple syrup
    - 1/4 cup (60 g) unsalted butter
    - 1/2 cup (60 g) powdered sugar
    - 1/2 teaspoon vanilla extract (optional)

Instructions:

1. **Prepare the Yeast Mixture:**
    - In a small bowl, combine the warm milk and granulated sugar. Sprinkle the yeast over the mixture and let it sit for about 5-10 minutes, or until frothy.
2. **Mix Brioche Dough:**
    - In a large mixing bowl or the bowl of a stand mixer fitted with the paddle attachment, beat the eggs. Add the yeast mixture and mix to combine.
    - Gradually add the softened butter and mix until combined.
    - Add the flour and salt, mixing until a dough forms. If using a stand mixer, switch to the dough hook attachment and knead on medium speed for about 8-10 minutes, or until the dough is smooth and elastic. If mixing by hand, knead on a floured surface.
3. **First Rise:**
    - Place the dough in a lightly greased bowl, cover it with plastic wrap or a damp cloth, and let it rise in a warm place for 1.5-2 hours, or until doubled in size.
4. **Shape the Brioche:**
    - Punch down the dough and turn it out onto a lightly floured surface. Shape it into a loaf or divide it into smaller portions for rolls.
    - Place the shaped dough into a greased loaf pan or onto a greased baking sheet. If making rolls, place them close together on the baking sheet.
5. **Second Rise:**
    - Cover the dough with a damp cloth or plastic wrap and let it rise again for about 30-45 minutes, or until puffed and nearly doubled.
6. **Preheat Oven:**

- Preheat your oven to 375°F (190°C).

7. **Bake the Brioche:**
   - Bake in the preheated oven for 25-35 minutes, or until the brioche is golden brown and sounds hollow when tapped on the bottom. The internal temperature should be about 190°F (88°C).

8. **Prepare the Maple Glaze:**
   - While the brioche is baking, make the glaze. In a small saucepan, melt the butter over medium heat. Stir in the maple syrup and bring to a simmer.
   - Remove from heat and whisk in the powdered sugar until smooth. If desired, add vanilla extract for extra flavor.

9. **Glaze the Brioche:**
   - Allow the brioche to cool for about 10 minutes before removing it from the pan. Brush the warm brioche with the maple glaze, making sure to coat it evenly.

10. **Cool and Serve:**
    - Let the brioche cool completely before slicing. The glaze will set as it cools.

Notes:

- **Butter:** Ensure the butter is softened to room temperature for easy incorporation into the dough.
- **Texture:** Brioche dough is rich and slightly sticky. It's important to knead it thoroughly to develop the gluten for a light, airy texture.
- **Glaze:** The maple glaze will harden slightly as it cools, giving the brioche a beautiful, glossy finish.

Storage: Store the cooled brioche in an airtight container at room temperature for up to 3 days. It can also be frozen for up to 1 month. Reheat gently in the oven or toaster to refresh.

Enjoy your Maple Glazed Brioche as a luxurious treat with coffee or tea, or as a delightful addition to any breakfast or brunch spread!

Pumpkin Seed Rye Bread

Ingredients:

- **For the Dough:**
    - 1 1/2 cups (360 ml) warm water (110°F/45°C)
    - 2 tablespoons (25 g) molasses or honey
    - 2 teaspoons (10 g) caraway seeds (optional, for added flavor)
    - 2 1/4 teaspoons (7 g) active dry yeast
    - 1 cup (120 g) rye flour
    - 2 1/2 cups (315 g) all-purpose flour
    - 1/2 cup (70 g) pumpkin seeds
    - 1 tablespoon (15 g) salt
- **For the Topping (optional):**
    - 1/4 cup (35 g) pumpkin seeds

Instructions:

1. **Activate the Yeast:**
    - In a small bowl, combine the warm water and molasses (or honey). Sprinkle the yeast over the mixture and let it sit for about 5-10 minutes, or until frothy.
2. **Mix Dough Ingredients:**
    - In a large mixing bowl or the bowl of a stand mixer, combine the rye flour and all-purpose flour. Stir in the caraway seeds (if using) and salt.
    - Make a well in the center of the flour mixture and pour in the yeast mixture. Mix until a dough forms.
    - Add the pumpkin seeds and mix until they are evenly distributed.
3. **Knead the Dough:**
    - Turn the dough out onto a lightly floured surface and knead for about 8-10 minutes, or until smooth and elastic. The dough should be slightly sticky but manageable.
4. **First Rise:**
    - Place the dough in a lightly oiled bowl, cover it with plastic wrap or a damp cloth, and let it rise in a warm place for 1-1.5 hours, or until doubled in size.
5. **Shape the Loaf:**
    - Punch down the dough and turn it out onto a lightly floured surface. Shape it into a loaf or divide it into smaller portions if you prefer mini loaves.
    - Place the shaped dough into a greased 9x5 inch (23x13 cm) loaf pan or onto a greased baking sheet.
6. **Prepare for Second Rise:**
    - Cover the dough with a damp cloth or plastic wrap and let it rise again for about 30-45 minutes, or until it has risen slightly above the edge of the pan or rolls are puffy.

7. **Preheat Oven:**
    - Preheat your oven to 375°F (190°C).
8. **Prepare for Baking:**
    - Brush the top of the loaf with a little water and sprinkle with additional pumpkin seeds if desired. This will give the bread a nice texture and appearance.
9. **Bake the Bread:**
    - Bake in the preheated oven for 30-35 minutes, or until the bread is golden brown and sounds hollow when tapped on the bottom. The internal temperature should be about 190°F (88°C).
10. **Cool:**
    - Allow the bread to cool in the pan for about 10 minutes before transferring it to a wire rack to cool completely.

Notes:

- **Rye Flour:** Rye flour gives the bread its distinctive flavor and denser texture. Combining it with all-purpose flour helps achieve a lighter loaf.
- **Pumpkin Seeds:** Roasting the pumpkin seeds lightly before adding them can enhance their flavor, but it's optional.
- **Texture:** Rye dough can be stickier than wheat dough. If it's too sticky, add a bit more flour as needed.

Storage: Store the cooled bread in an airtight container at room temperature for up to 3 days. It can also be frozen for up to 3 months. To refresh, toast slices or warm the loaf in the oven.

Enjoy your Pumpkin Seed Rye Bread as a hearty, nutritious option for sandwiches or alongside your favorite soups and stews!

Cornmeal Muffins

Ingredients:

- **Dry Ingredients:**
    - 1 cup (120 g) cornmeal
    - 1 cup (125 g) all-purpose flour
    - 1/4 cup (50 g) granulated sugar
    - 1 tablespoon (15 g) baking powder
    - 1/2 teaspoon (2.5 g) salt
- **Wet Ingredients:**
    - 1 cup (240 ml) milk
    - 1/4 cup (60 ml) vegetable oil or melted butter
    - 2 large eggs
    - 1 tablespoon (15 ml) honey or maple syrup (optional, for added sweetness)

Optional Add-Ins:

- 1/2 cup (75 g) shredded cheese (e.g., cheddar or Monterey Jack)
- 1/2 cup (75 g) cooked and crumbled bacon
- 1/2 cup (80 g) fresh or frozen corn kernels
- 1/4 cup (30 g) chopped jalapeños or green chilies for a spicy kick

Instructions:

1. **Preheat Oven:**
    - Preheat your oven to 400°F (200°C). Line a muffin tin with paper liners or lightly grease the cups.
2. **Mix Dry Ingredients:**
    - In a large mixing bowl, whisk together the cornmeal, all-purpose flour, granulated sugar, baking powder, and salt.
3. **Mix Wet Ingredients:**
    - In a separate bowl, whisk together the milk, vegetable oil (or melted butter), eggs, and honey (if using).
4. **Combine Ingredients:**
    - Pour the wet ingredients into the dry ingredients and stir gently until just combined. The batter will be a bit lumpy; do not overmix.
5. **Add Optional Ingredients:**
    - If you are adding cheese, bacon, corn kernels, or jalapeños, gently fold them into the batter.
6. **Fill Muffin Cups:**
    - Divide the batter evenly among the muffin cups, filling each about 2/3 full.
7. **Bake Muffins:**
    - Bake in the preheated oven for 15-20 minutes, or until the muffins are golden brown and a toothpick inserted into the center comes out clean.
8. **Cool:**

- Allow the muffins to cool in the tin for 5 minutes, then transfer them to a wire rack to cool completely.

Notes:

- **Texture:** The cornmeal gives these muffins a slightly gritty texture, which is characteristic of cornbread. If you prefer a finer texture, you can use a finer cornmeal.
- **Sweetness:** Adjust the amount of sugar based on your preference. For a less sweet muffin, you can reduce or omit the sugar.
- **Storage:** Store the cooled muffins in an airtight container at room temperature for up to 3 days. They can also be frozen for up to 3 months. To refresh, warm them in the oven or toaster.

Serving Suggestions: Enjoy these cornmeal muffins as a side with soups, stews, or chili, or simply spread with a bit of butter or honey for a tasty snack.

Enjoy your homemade Cornmeal Muffins!

Sour Cherry Rye Bread

Ingredients:

- **For the Dough:**
    - 1 1/2 cups (360 ml) warm water (110°F/45°C)
    - 2 tablespoons (25 g) honey or molasses
    - 2 1/4 teaspoons (7 g) active dry yeast
    - 1 cup (120 g) rye flour
    - 2 1/2 cups (315 g) all-purpose flour
    - 1 teaspoon (5 g) caraway seeds (optional, for added flavor)
    - 1 cup (150 g) dried sour cherries, chopped
    - 1 tablespoon (15 g) salt
- **For the Topping (optional):**
    - 1/4 cup (30 g) chopped dried sour cherries
    - 1 tablespoon (15 g) all-purpose flour (for dusting)

Instructions:

1. **Activate the Yeast:**
    - In a small bowl, combine the warm water and honey (or molasses). Sprinkle the yeast over the mixture and let it sit for about 5-10 minutes, or until frothy.
2. **Prepare the Dough:**
    - In a large mixing bowl or the bowl of a stand mixer, combine the rye flour and all-purpose flour. Stir in the caraway seeds (if using) and salt.
    - Make a well in the center of the flour mixture and pour in the yeast mixture. Mix until a dough starts to form.
    - Add the chopped dried sour cherries and mix until evenly distributed.
3. **Knead the Dough:**
    - Turn the dough out onto a lightly floured surface and knead for about 8-10 minutes, or until smooth and elastic. The dough should be slightly sticky but manageable.
4. **First Rise:**
    - Place the dough in a lightly oiled bowl, cover it with plastic wrap or a damp cloth, and let it rise in a warm place for 1-1.5 hours, or until doubled in size.
5. **Shape the Loaf:**
    - Punch down the dough and turn it out onto a lightly floured surface. Shape it into a loaf or divide it into smaller portions if you prefer mini loaves.
    - Place the shaped dough into a greased 9x5 inch (23x13 cm) loaf pan or onto a greased baking sheet.
6. **Prepare for Second Rise:**

- Cover the dough with a damp cloth or plastic wrap and let it rise again for about 30-45 minutes, or until it has risen slightly above the edge of the pan or rolls are puffy.

7. **Preheat Oven:**
   - Preheat your oven to 375°F (190°C).
8. **Prepare for Baking:**
   - If desired, brush the top of the loaf with a little water and sprinkle with additional chopped dried sour cherries and a dusting of flour for added texture and appearance.
9. **Bake the Bread:**
   - Bake in the preheated oven for 30-35 minutes, or until the bread is golden brown and sounds hollow when tapped on the bottom. The internal temperature should be about 190°F (88°C).
10. **Cool:**
    - Allow the bread to cool in the pan for about 10 minutes before transferring it to a wire rack to cool completely.

Notes:

- **Sour Cherries:** If using fresh sour cherries, be sure to pit and chop them, and you may need to adjust the amount of water in the dough slightly due to the added moisture.
- **Texture:** Rye dough is typically denser and more sticky than wheat dough. It's important to knead it thoroughly for a good texture.
- **Flavor:** Caraway seeds add a traditional flavor to rye bread, but they can be omitted if preferred.

Storage: Store the cooled bread in an airtight container at room temperature for up to 3 days. It can also be frozen for up to 3 months. To refresh, toast slices or warm the loaf in the oven.

Enjoy your homemade Sour Cherry Rye Bread as a unique and delicious addition to your baking repertoire!

Cranberry Orange Bread

Ingredients:

- **For the Bread:**
    - 1/2 cup (120 ml) orange juice
    - 1/2 cup (115 g) unsalted butter, softened
    - 1 cup (200 g) granulated sugar
    - 2 large eggs
    - 1 tablespoon (15 ml) grated orange zest (about 1 orange)
    - 2 cups (250 g) all-purpose flour
    - 1 1/2 teaspoons (6 g) baking powder
    - 1/2 teaspoon (2.5 g) baking soda
    - 1/2 teaspoon (2.5 g) salt
    - 1 1/2 cups (150 g) fresh or frozen cranberries, coarsely chopped
- **For the Glaze (optional):**
    - 1/2 cup (60 g) powdered sugar
    - 2 tablespoons (30 ml) orange juice

Instructions:

1. **Preheat Oven:**
    - Preheat your oven to 350°F (175°C). Grease and flour a 9x5 inch (23x13 cm) loaf pan, or line it with parchment paper.
2. **Mix Wet Ingredients:**
    - In a medium bowl, beat together the softened butter and granulated sugar until light and fluffy.
    - Add the eggs, one at a time, beating well after each addition.
    - Stir in the orange juice and grated orange zest until combined.
3. **Mix Dry Ingredients:**
    - In a separate bowl, whisk together the all-purpose flour, baking powder, baking soda, and salt.
4. **Combine Ingredients:**
    - Gradually add the dry ingredients to the wet ingredients, mixing until just combined.
    - Gently fold in the chopped cranberries. Be careful not to overmix, as this can make the bread dense.
5. **Transfer to Pan:**
    - Pour the batter into the prepared loaf pan and smooth the top with a spatula.
6. **Bake the Bread:**
    - Bake in the preheated oven for 55-65 minutes, or until a toothpick inserted into the center of the loaf comes out clean. The top should be golden brown and the loaf should have risen.

7. **Cool:**
    - Allow the bread to cool in the pan for about 10 minutes before transferring it to a wire rack to cool completely.
8. **Prepare the Glaze (Optional):**
    - If you're using a glaze, whisk together the powdered sugar and orange juice in a small bowl until smooth.
    - Drizzle the glaze over the cooled bread.

Notes:

- **Cranberries:** If using frozen cranberries, do not thaw them before adding to the batter. This helps to prevent the batter from turning pink.
- **Texture:** The bread will have a slightly dense crumb due to the fruit, but it should still be moist and tender.
- **Orange Zest:** For a more intense orange flavor, you can add additional zest or use orange extract.

Storage: Store the cooled bread in an airtight container at room temperature for up to 4 days. It can also be frozen for up to 3 months. To refresh, toast slices or warm the loaf in the oven.

Enjoy your Cranberry Orange Bread as a delightful and flavorful addition to any meal or as a special treat on its own!

Canadian Caramelized Onion Bread

Ingredients:

- **For the Caramelized Onions:**
    - 2 large onions, thinly sliced
    - 2 tablespoons (30 ml) olive oil
    - 1 tablespoon (15 g) unsalted butter
    - 1/2 teaspoon (2.5 g) salt
    - 1 teaspoon (5 g) sugar (optional, for extra sweetness)
- **For the Bread Dough:**
    - 1 cup (240 ml) warm water (110°F/45°C)
    - 2 tablespoons (25 g) honey
    - 2 1/4 teaspoons (7 g) active dry yeast
    - 3 cups (375 g) all-purpose flour
    - 1 cup (120 g) whole wheat flour
    - 1 teaspoon (5 g) salt
    - 2 tablespoons (30 ml) olive oil

Instructions:

1. **Caramelize the Onions:**
    - In a large skillet, heat the olive oil and butter over medium heat.
    - Add the sliced onions and salt. Cook, stirring occasionally, for about 15-20 minutes, or until the onions are golden brown and caramelized.
    - If desired, add the sugar to enhance the sweetness. Continue cooking for an additional 5 minutes.
    - Remove from heat and let cool.
2. **Activate the Yeast:**
    - In a small bowl, combine the warm water and honey. Sprinkle the yeast over the mixture and let it sit for about 5-10 minutes, or until frothy.
3. **Mix the Dough:**
    - In a large mixing bowl or the bowl of a stand mixer, combine the all-purpose flour, whole wheat flour, and salt.
    - Make a well in the center and pour in the yeast mixture and olive oil. Mix until a dough starts to form.
    - Turn the dough out onto a floured surface and knead for about 8-10 minutes, or until smooth and elastic.
4. **Incorporate the Caramelized Onions:**
    - Gently fold the caramelized onions into the dough until evenly distributed.
5. **First Rise:**
    - Place the dough in a lightly oiled bowl, cover it with plastic wrap or a damp cloth, and let it rise in a warm place for about 1-1.5 hours, or until doubled in size.

6. **Shape the Loaf:**
    - Punch down the dough and turn it out onto a lightly floured surface. Shape it into a loaf or divide it into smaller portions for mini loaves.
    - Place the shaped dough into a greased 9x5 inch (23x13 cm) loaf pan or onto a greased baking sheet.
7. **Prepare for Second Rise:**
    - Cover the dough with a damp cloth or plastic wrap and let it rise again for about 30-45 minutes, or until it has risen slightly above the edge of the pan or rolls are puffy.
8. **Preheat Oven:**
    - Preheat your oven to 375°F (190°C).
9. **Bake the Bread:**
    - Bake in the preheated oven for 30-35 minutes, or until the bread is golden brown and sounds hollow when tapped on the bottom. The internal temperature should be about 190°F (88°C).
10. **Cool:**
    - Allow the bread to cool in the pan for about 10 minutes before transferring it to a wire rack to cool completely.

Notes:

- **Onion Preparation:** Caramelizing the onions adds depth and sweetness to the bread. Make sure the onions are well caramelized for the best flavor.
- **Texture:** The whole wheat flour adds a bit of texture and nuttiness. If you prefer a lighter bread, you can use all-purpose flour.
- **Variations:** You can add herbs such as thyme or rosemary to the dough for extra flavor.

Storage: Store the cooled bread in an airtight container at room temperature for up to 4 days. It can also be frozen for up to 3 months. To refresh, toast slices or warm the loaf in the oven.

Enjoy your Canadian Caramelized Onion Bread as a flavorful and aromatic addition to your meals!

Herb and Cheese Pull-Apart Bread

Ingredients:

- **For the Dough:**
    - 1 cup (240 ml) warm milk (110°F/45°C)
    - 1/4 cup (60 ml) warm water (110°F/45°C)
    - 1/4 cup (50 g) granulated sugar
    - 2 1/4 teaspoons (7 g) active dry yeast
    - 1/4 cup (60 g) unsalted butter, melted
    - 1 large egg
    - 3 1/2 cups (440 g) all-purpose flour
    - 1 teaspoon (5 g) salt
- **For the Filling:**
    - 1 cup (100 g) shredded mozzarella cheese
    - 1/2 cup (50 g) shredded cheddar cheese
    - 1/4 cup (60 g) grated Parmesan cheese
    - 2 tablespoons (30 g) unsalted butter, melted
    - 2 tablespoons (15 g) chopped fresh parsley (or 1 tablespoon dried parsley)
    - 1 tablespoon (15 g) chopped fresh chives (or 1 teaspoon dried chives)
    - 1 tablespoon (15 g) chopped fresh rosemary (or 1 teaspoon dried rosemary)
    - 1/2 teaspoon (2.5 g) garlic powder

Instructions:

1. **Activate the Yeast:**
    - In a small bowl, combine the warm milk, warm water, and granulated sugar. Sprinkle the yeast over the mixture and let it sit for about 5-10 minutes, or until frothy.
2. **Mix the Dough:**
    - In a large mixing bowl or the bowl of a stand mixer, combine 3 cups of all-purpose flour and salt. Make a well in the center and add the yeast mixture, melted butter, and egg. Mix until a dough forms.
    - Gradually add the remaining flour, 1/4 cup at a time, until the dough is soft and slightly sticky but manageable.
3. **Knead the Dough:**
    - Turn the dough out onto a lightly floured surface and knead for about 8-10 minutes, or until smooth and elastic.
4. **First Rise:**
    - Place the dough in a lightly oiled bowl, cover it with plastic wrap or a damp cloth, and let it rise in a warm place for about 1-1.5 hours, or until doubled in size.
5. **Prepare the Filling:**

- In a small bowl, mix together the melted butter, chopped parsley, chives, rosemary, and garlic powder.
6. **Shape the Bread:**
    - Punch down the dough and turn it out onto a lightly floured surface. Roll it into a rectangle about 12x16 inches (30x40 cm).
    - Brush the dough with the herb butter mixture. Sprinkle the shredded mozzarella, cheddar, and Parmesan cheese evenly over the dough.
7. **Cut and Stack:**
    - Cut the dough into squares, about 3x3 inches (7.5x7.5 cm). Stack the squares in a greased 9x5 inch (23x13 cm) loaf pan, placing them vertically.
8. **Second Rise:**
    - Cover the pan with a damp cloth and let the dough rise for about 30-45 minutes, or until puffy and nearly doubled in size.
9. **Preheat Oven:**
    - Preheat your oven to 375°F (190°C).
10. **Bake the Bread:**
    - Bake in the preheated oven for 30-35 minutes, or until the bread is golden brown and cooked through. The internal temperature should be around 190°F (88°C).
11. **Cool and Serve:**
    - Allow the bread to cool in the pan for about 10 minutes before transferring it to a wire rack to cool slightly. Serve warm or at room temperature.

Notes:

- **Cheese Varieties:** Feel free to use different types of cheese according to your taste. Gruyère, fontina, or gouda are great alternatives.
- **Herbs:** Fresh herbs provide the best flavor, but dried herbs can be used if fresh are not available.
- **Storage:** Store leftover bread in an airtight container at room temperature for up to 3 days. It can also be frozen for up to 3 months. To refresh, reheat in the oven.

Enjoy your Herb and Cheese Pull-Apart Bread as a delicious, cheesy, and herb-infused treat that's perfect for any occasion!

Wild Berry Buttermilk Muffins

Ingredients:

- **For the Muffins:**
    - 2 1/2 cups (315 g) all-purpose flour
    - 1 cup (200 g) granulated sugar
    - 1 tablespoon (15 g) baking powder
    - 1/2 teaspoon (2.5 g) baking soda
    - 1/2 teaspoon (2.5 g) salt
    - 1/2 cup (115 g) unsalted butter, melted and slightly cooled
    - 1 cup (240 ml) buttermilk
    - 2 large eggs
    - 1 teaspoon (5 ml) vanilla extract
    - 1 1/2 cups (225 g) wild berries (such as blueberries, raspberries, blackberries, or a mix)
- **For the Topping (optional):**
    - 2 tablespoons (25 g) granulated sugar
    - 1/2 teaspoon (2.5 g) ground cinnamon

Instructions:

1. **Preheat Oven:**
    - Preheat your oven to 375°F (190°C). Line a 12-cup muffin tin with paper liners or grease the cups lightly.
2. **Prepare the Dry Ingredients:**
    - In a large mixing bowl, whisk together the all-purpose flour, granulated sugar, baking powder, baking soda, and salt.
3. **Mix the Wet Ingredients:**
    - In another bowl, whisk together the melted butter, buttermilk, eggs, and vanilla extract until well combined.
4. **Combine Wet and Dry Ingredients:**
    - Pour the wet ingredients into the dry ingredients. Gently fold them together using a spatula or wooden spoon until just combined. Be careful not to overmix; a few lumps are okay.
5. **Add the Berries:**
    - Gently fold in the wild berries. If using frozen berries, do not thaw them; fold them in while still frozen to prevent bleeding into the batter.
6. **Fill the Muffin Tin:**
    - Divide the batter evenly among the muffin cups, filling each about 2/3 full.
7. **Prepare the Topping (Optional):**
    - If using, mix the granulated sugar and ground cinnamon in a small bowl. Sprinkle a pinch of this mixture over the top of each muffin before baking.

8. **Bake the Muffins:**
   - Bake in the preheated oven for 18-22 minutes, or until a toothpick inserted into the center of a muffin comes out clean. The tops should be golden brown.
9. **Cool:**
   - Allow the muffins to cool in the tin for about 5 minutes before transferring them to a wire rack to cool completely.

Notes:

- **Berry Variations:** Feel free to use a mix of berries or your favorite type of wild berries. Fresh or frozen berries work well, but avoid thawing frozen berries to prevent excessive bleeding into the batter.
- **Buttermilk Substitute:** If you don't have buttermilk, you can use milk with a tablespoon of lemon juice or white vinegar, letting it sit for 5 minutes to sour.
- **Texture:** For a tender muffin, be sure not to overmix the batter once the wet and dry ingredients are combined.

Storage: Store the cooled muffins in an airtight container at room temperature for up to 3 days. They can also be frozen for up to 3 months. To refresh, reheat in the oven or microwave.

Enjoy your Wild Berry Buttermilk Muffins as a delicious and satisfying treat!

Alberta Grain Bread

Ingredients:

- **For the Soaked Grains:**
    - 1/2 cup (80 g) rolled oats
    - 1/2 cup (80 g) cracked wheat or bulgur
    - 1/4 cup (30 g) sunflower seeds
    - 1/4 cup (30 g) pumpkin seeds
    - 1/4 cup (30 g) flaxseeds
    - 1 cup (240 ml) boiling water
- **For the Bread Dough:**
    - 1 cup (240 ml) warm water (110°F/45°C)
    - 2 tablespoons (25 g) honey
    - 2 1/4 teaspoons (7 g) active dry yeast
    - 1/4 cup (60 ml) olive oil or canola oil
    - 1/2 cup (120 ml) buttermilk or milk
    - 1 cup (130 g) whole wheat flour
    - 2 cups (250 g) all-purpose flour
    - 1 teaspoon (5 g) salt
- **For the Topping (optional):**
    - 1 tablespoon (10 g) rolled oats
    - 1 tablespoon (10 g) sunflower seeds

Instructions:

1. **Soak the Grains:**
    - In a medium bowl, combine the rolled oats, cracked wheat, sunflower seeds, pumpkin seeds, and flaxseeds.
    - Pour the boiling water over the mixture and stir to combine. Cover and let sit for about 30 minutes, or until the grains have absorbed the water and are soft.
2. **Activate the Yeast:**
    - In a small bowl, combine the warm water and honey. Sprinkle the yeast over the mixture and let it sit for about 5-10 minutes, or until frothy.
3. **Mix the Dough:**
    - In a large mixing bowl or the bowl of a stand mixer, combine the whole wheat flour and salt.
    - Make a well in the center and add the yeast mixture, olive oil, and buttermilk. Mix until a dough starts to form.
    - Gradually add the all-purpose flour, 1/4 cup at a time, until the dough is soft and slightly sticky but manageable.
4. **Incorporate the Soaked Grains:**
    - Gently fold the soaked grains mixture into the dough until evenly distributed.

5. **Knead the Dough:**
   - Turn the dough out onto a floured surface and knead for about 8-10 minutes, or until smooth and elastic.
6. **First Rise:**
   - Place the dough in a lightly oiled bowl, cover it with plastic wrap or a damp cloth, and let it rise in a warm place for about 1-1.5 hours, or until doubled in size.
7. **Shape the Loaf:**
   - Punch down the dough and turn it out onto a lightly floured surface. Shape it into a loaf or divide it into smaller portions for mini loaves.
   - Place the shaped dough into a greased 9x5 inch (23x13 cm) loaf pan or onto a greased baking sheet.
8. **Prepare for Second Rise:**
   - Cover the dough with a damp cloth or plastic wrap and let it rise again for about 30-45 minutes, or until it has risen slightly above the edge of the pan or rolls are puffy.
9. **Preheat Oven:**
   - Preheat your oven to 375°F (190°C).
10. **Bake the Bread:**
    - If using, sprinkle the rolled oats and sunflower seeds on top of the dough before baking.
    - Bake in the preheated oven for 30-35 minutes, or until the bread is golden brown and sounds hollow when tapped on the bottom. The internal temperature should be around 190°F (88°C).
11. **Cool:**
    - Allow the bread to cool in the pan for about 10 minutes before transferring it to a wire rack to cool completely.

Notes:

- **Grain Variations:** You can customize the grain mix to your preference or availability. Other grains such as quinoa, barley, or millet can be used.
- **Texture:** The bread will have a hearty and dense texture due to the variety of grains. It's excellent for sandwiches or as a side with soups and stews.
- **Storage:** Store the cooled bread in an airtight container at room temperature for up to 4 days. It can also be frozen for up to 3 months. To refresh, toast slices or warm the loaf in the oven.

Enjoy your Alberta Grain Bread as a nutritious and flavorful addition to your meals!

Lemon Poppy Seed Loaf

Ingredients:

- **For the Loaf:**
    - 1 1/2 cups (190 g) all-purpose flour
    - 1/2 cup (100 g) granulated sugar
    - 1 tablespoon (15 g) baking powder
    - 1/2 teaspoon (2.5 g) salt
    - 1/4 cup (60 ml) vegetable oil or melted butter
    - 1/2 cup (120 ml) milk
    - 2 large eggs
    - Zest of 2 large lemons
    - 2 tablespoons (20 g) poppy seeds
    - 2 tablespoons (30 ml) fresh lemon juice
- **For the Lemon Glaze:**
    - 1 cup (120 g) powdered sugar
    - 2 tablespoons (30 ml) fresh lemon juice
    - 1 tablespoon (15 g) unsalted butter, melted (optional for extra richness)

Instructions:

1. **Preheat Oven:**
    - Preheat your oven to 350°F (175°C). Grease and flour a 9x5 inch (23x13 cm) loaf pan, or line it with parchment paper.
2. **Mix Dry Ingredients:**
    - In a large bowl, whisk together the all-purpose flour, granulated sugar, baking powder, and salt.
3. **Mix Wet Ingredients:**
    - In another bowl, whisk together the vegetable oil, milk, eggs, lemon zest, poppy seeds, and lemon juice until well combined.
4. **Combine Ingredients:**
    - Pour the wet ingredients into the dry ingredients. Gently fold them together until just combined. Be careful not to overmix; the batter should be slightly lumpy.
5. **Pour into Pan:**
    - Pour the batter into the prepared loaf pan and spread it evenly.
6. **Bake the Loaf:**
    - Bake in the preheated oven for 50-60 minutes, or until a toothpick inserted into the center of the loaf comes out clean. The top should be golden brown.
7. **Cool:**
    - Allow the loaf to cool in the pan for about 10 minutes before transferring it to a wire rack to cool completely.
8. **Prepare the Glaze:**

- In a small bowl, whisk together the powdered sugar, lemon juice, and melted butter (if using) until smooth and well combined.
9. **Glaze the Loaf:**
    - Once the loaf is completely cool, drizzle the lemon glaze over the top, allowing it to drip down the sides.

Notes:

- **Lemon Zest:** For the best flavor, use fresh lemon zest. It provides a bright, aromatic quality to the loaf.
- **Poppy Seeds:** Ensure that you use fresh poppy seeds for the best texture and flavor.
- **Storage:** Store the cooled loaf in an airtight container at room temperature for up to 4 days. It can also be frozen for up to 3 months. To refresh, let it thaw at room temperature or warm it slightly in the oven.

Enjoy your Lemon Poppy Seed Loaf with a cup of tea or coffee for a refreshing and delightful treat!

Canadian Bacon and Cheese Bread

Ingredients:

- **For the Dough:**
    - 1 cup (240 ml) warm milk (110°F/45°C)
    - 2 tablespoons (25 g) granulated sugar
    - 2 1/4 teaspoons (7 g) active dry yeast
    - 1/4 cup (60 g) unsalted butter, melted
    - 1 large egg
    - 3 cups (375 g) all-purpose flour
    - 1 teaspoon (5 g) salt
- **For the Filling:**
    - 1 cup (150 g) shredded cheddar cheese
    - 1 cup (120 g) shredded mozzarella cheese
    - 1 cup (150 g) diced Canadian bacon
    - 2 tablespoons (30 g) finely chopped fresh chives (optional)
    - 1/2 teaspoon (2.5 g) garlic powder (optional)
- **For the Topping (optional):**
    - 1/4 cup (25 g) shredded cheddar cheese
    - 1 tablespoon (15 g) chopped fresh chives

Instructions:

1. **Activate the Yeast:**
    - In a small bowl, combine the warm milk and granulated sugar. Sprinkle the yeast over the mixture and let it sit for about 5-10 minutes, or until frothy.
2. **Mix the Dough:**
    - In a large bowl or the bowl of a stand mixer, combine the flour and salt.
    - Make a well in the center and add the yeast mixture, melted butter, and egg. Mix until a dough starts to form.
    - Knead the dough on a floured surface or with the dough hook attachment of your stand mixer for about 8-10 minutes, or until smooth and elastic.
3. **First Rise:**
    - Place the dough in a lightly oiled bowl, cover it with plastic wrap or a damp cloth, and let it rise in a warm place for about 1-1.5 hours, or until doubled in size.
4. **Prepare the Filling:**
    - While the dough is rising, mix the shredded cheddar cheese, shredded mozzarella cheese, diced Canadian bacon, and finely chopped chives (if using) in a bowl. Add garlic powder if desired.
5. **Shape the Bread:**
    - Punch down the dough and turn it out onto a floured surface. Roll it into a rectangle about 12x16 inches (30x40 cm).

- Evenly spread the cheese and bacon mixture over the dough.
- Roll the dough up tightly from one long side, like a jelly roll, and pinch the seams to seal. Place the roll seam-side down in a greased 9x5 inch (23x13 cm) loaf pan.
6. **Second Rise:**
   - Cover the pan with a damp cloth or plastic wrap and let the dough rise for another 30-45 minutes, or until puffy and nearly doubled in size.
7. **Preheat Oven:**
   - Preheat your oven to 375°F (190°C).
8. **Bake the Bread:**
   - If using, sprinkle the top of the loaf with the additional shredded cheddar cheese and chopped chives.
   - Bake in the preheated oven for 30-35 minutes, or until the bread is golden brown and sounds hollow when tapped on the bottom. The internal temperature should be around 190°F (88°C).
9. **Cool:**
   - Allow the bread to cool in the pan for about 10 minutes before transferring it to a wire rack to cool completely.

Notes:

- **Cheese Variations:** Feel free to use different types of cheese based on your preference, such as gouda, fontina, or pepper jack for a spicier kick.
- **Canadian Bacon:** If Canadian bacon is not available, you can substitute with regular bacon, cooked and crumbled.
- **Storage:** Store the cooled bread in an airtight container at room temperature for up to 4 days. It can also be frozen for up to 3 months. To refresh, warm in the oven or toaster.

Enjoy your Canadian Bacon and Cheese Bread as a delicious and flavorful addition to your meals!

Saskatoon Berry and Almond Bread

Ingredients:

- **For the Bread:**
    - 1/2 cup (115 g) unsalted butter, softened
    - 1 cup (200 g) granulated sugar
    - 2 large eggs
    - 1 cup (240 ml) buttermilk or milk
    - 1 teaspoon (5 ml) vanilla extract
    - 2 cups (250 g) all-purpose flour
    - 1 1/2 teaspoons (6 g) baking powder
    - 1/2 teaspoon (2.5 g) baking soda
    - 1/4 teaspoon (1.25 g) salt
    - 1 cup (150 g) fresh or frozen Saskatoon berries (if frozen, do not thaw)
    - 1/2 cup (50 g) sliced almonds
- **For the Topping (optional):**
    - 2 tablespoons (25 g) granulated sugar
    - 1/4 cup (25 g) sliced almonds

Instructions:

1. **Preheat Oven:**
    - Preheat your oven to 350°F (175°C). Grease and flour a 9x5 inch (23x13 cm) loaf pan or line it with parchment paper.
2. **Prepare the Batter:**
    - In a large bowl, cream together the softened butter and granulated sugar until light and fluffy.
    - Beat in the eggs one at a time, ensuring each egg is fully incorporated before adding the next.
    - Stir in the buttermilk and vanilla extract.
3. **Combine Dry Ingredients:**
    - In a separate bowl, whisk together the all-purpose flour, baking powder, baking soda, and salt.
4. **Mix Wet and Dry Ingredients:**
    - Gradually add the dry ingredients to the wet ingredients, mixing just until combined. Be careful not to overmix; the batter should be slightly lumpy.
    - Gently fold in the Saskatoon berries. If using frozen berries, fold them in gently to prevent bleeding into the batter.
5. **Pour into Pan:**
    - Pour the batter into the prepared loaf pan, spreading it evenly.
6. **Prepare the Topping (Optional):**

- In a small bowl, mix together the granulated sugar and sliced almonds. Sprinkle this mixture evenly over the top of the batter.
7. **Bake the Bread:**
   - Bake in the preheated oven for 55-65 minutes, or until a toothpick inserted into the center of the loaf comes out clean. The top should be golden brown.
8. **Cool:**
   - Allow the bread to cool in the pan for about 10 minutes before transferring it to a wire rack to cool completely.

Notes:

- **Saskatoon Berries:** If you can't find Saskatoon berries, you can substitute with blueberries or blackberries, though the flavor will be different.
- **Almond Variations:** For added texture, you can use chopped almonds instead of sliced almonds.
- **Buttermilk Substitute:** If you don't have buttermilk, you can use milk mixed with a tablespoon of lemon juice or white vinegar, letting it sit for 5 minutes to sour.
- **Storage:** Store the cooled bread in an airtight container at room temperature for up to 4 days. It can also be frozen for up to 3 months. To refresh, let it thaw at room temperature or warm it slightly in the oven.

Enjoy your Saskatoon Berry and Almond Bread as a delicious and unique treat that combines the best of both sweet and nutty flavors!

Maple-Glazed Pretzel Bites

Ingredients:

- **For the Pretzel Bites:**
    - 1 1/2 cups (360 ml) warm water (110°F/45°C)
    - 1/4 cup (50 g) granulated sugar
    - 2 1/4 teaspoons (7 g) active dry yeast
    - 3 1/2 cups (440 g) all-purpose flour
    - 1 teaspoon (5 g) salt
    - 1/4 cup (60 g) baking soda (for boiling)
    - Coarse sea salt (for sprinkling)
- **For the Maple Glaze:**
    - 1/2 cup (120 ml) pure maple syrup
    - 2 tablespoons (30 g) unsalted butter
    - 1 tablespoon (15 ml) water
    - 1 tablespoon (15 g) light corn syrup (optional, for extra shine)
    - 1/2 teaspoon (2.5 g) vanilla extract

Instructions:

1. **Prepare the Dough:**
    - In a large bowl, combine the warm water and granulated sugar. Sprinkle the yeast over the top and let it sit for about 5-10 minutes, or until frothy.
    - Add the flour and salt to the yeast mixture. Stir until a dough starts to form. Turn the dough out onto a floured surface and knead for about 8 minutes, or until smooth and elastic.
    - Place the dough in a lightly oiled bowl, cover with plastic wrap or a damp cloth, and let it rise in a warm place for about 1 hour, or until doubled in size.
2. **Shape the Pretzel Bites:**
    - Preheat your oven to 425°F (220°C). Line two baking sheets with parchment paper.
    - Punch down the dough and turn it out onto a floured surface. Roll it into a rectangle about 12x16 inches (30x40 cm). Cut the dough into small bite-sized pieces, approximately 1-inch squares.
3. **Boil the Pretzel Bites:**
    - In a large pot, bring 8 cups (2 liters) of water to a boil. Stir in the baking soda.
    - Drop the pretzel bites into the boiling water in batches, boiling for about 30 seconds per batch. Remove with a slotted spoon and place on the prepared baking sheets. Sprinkle with coarse sea salt.
4. **Bake the Pretzel Bites:**
    - Bake in the preheated oven for 12-15 minutes, or until golden brown.
5. **Prepare the Maple Glaze:**

- While the pretzel bites are baking, combine the maple syrup, butter, water, and light corn syrup (if using) in a small saucepan.
- Bring to a simmer over medium heat and cook, stirring occasionally, until the glaze has thickened slightly, about 5-7 minutes.
- Remove from heat and stir in the vanilla extract.

6. **Glaze the Pretzel Bites:**
   - Once the pretzel bites are done baking and still warm, brush them generously with the maple glaze.
7. **Cool:**
   - Allow the glazed pretzel bites to cool slightly before serving.

Notes:

- **Maple Syrup:** Use pure maple syrup for the best flavor. The light corn syrup helps give the glaze a shinier finish but can be omitted if not available.
- **Storage:** Store any leftover pretzel bites in an airtight container at room temperature for up to 2 days. They are best enjoyed fresh but can be reheated in a warm oven to refresh them.
- **Make Ahead:** You can prepare the pretzel bites up to the boiling stage, then freeze them. When ready to bake, simply thaw and bake from frozen, adding a few extra minutes to the baking time.

Enjoy your Maple-Glazed Pretzel Bites as a sweet and savory treat that's sure to be a hit with everyone!

Flaxseed and Sunflower Seed Bread

Ingredients:

- **For the Dough:**
    - 1 cup (240 ml) warm water (110°F/45°C)
    - 2 tablespoons (25 g) granulated sugar or honey
    - 2 1/4 teaspoons (7 g) active dry yeast
    - 2 tablespoons (30 ml) olive oil or melted butter
    - 1 large egg
    - 1 1/2 cups (190 g) whole wheat flour
    - 1 1/2 cups (190 g) all-purpose flour
    - 1/4 cup (25 g) ground flaxseeds
    - 1/4 cup (30 g) sunflower seeds
    - 1 teaspoon (5 g) salt
- **For the Topping (optional):**
    - 2 tablespoons (15 g) sunflower seeds
    - 1 tablespoon (10 g) ground flaxseeds

Instructions:

1. **Prepare the Yeast Mixture:**
    - In a large bowl, combine the warm water and granulated sugar or honey. Sprinkle the yeast over the top and let it sit for about 5-10 minutes, or until frothy.
2. **Mix the Dough:**
    - Add the olive oil (or melted butter) and egg to the yeast mixture. Stir to combine.
    - In another bowl, whisk together the whole wheat flour, all-purpose flour, ground flaxseeds, sunflower seeds, and salt.
    - Gradually add the dry ingredients to the wet ingredients, mixing until a dough forms.
3. **Knead the Dough:**
    - Turn the dough out onto a floured surface and knead for about 8-10 minutes, or until smooth and elastic. You can also use a stand mixer with a dough hook attachment for this step.
4. **First Rise:**
    - Place the dough in a lightly oiled bowl, cover it with plastic wrap or a damp cloth, and let it rise in a warm place for about 1 hour, or until doubled in size.
5. **Shape the Loaf:**
    - Punch down the dough and turn it out onto a floured surface. Shape the dough into a loaf and place it in a greased 9x5 inch (23x13 cm) loaf pan.
6. **Second Rise:**
    - Cover the pan with a damp cloth or plastic wrap and let the dough rise for an additional 30-45 minutes, or until puffy and nearly doubled.

7. **Preheat Oven:**
   - Preheat your oven to 375°F (190°C).
8. **Add Topping (Optional):**
   - If using, sprinkle the top of the loaf with the additional sunflower seeds and ground flaxseeds for extra texture and flavor.
9. **Bake the Bread:**
   - Bake in the preheated oven for 30-35 minutes, or until the bread is golden brown and sounds hollow when tapped on the bottom. The internal temperature should be around 190°F (88°C).
10. **Cool:**
    - Allow the bread to cool in the pan for about 10 minutes before transferring it to a wire rack to cool completely.

Notes:

- **Seed Variations:** Feel free to add other seeds or nuts, such as chia seeds, pumpkin seeds, or sesame seeds, for added texture and flavor.
- **Flaxseeds:** If you prefer, you can use whole flaxseeds instead of ground flaxseeds. Just be aware that ground flaxseeds are more easily digestible and blend more seamlessly into the dough.
- **Storage:** Store the cooled bread in an airtight container at room temperature for up to 4 days. It can also be frozen for up to 3 months. To refresh, let it thaw at room temperature or warm it slightly in the oven.

Enjoy your homemade Flaxseed and Sunflower Seed Bread as a wholesome and tasty addition to any meal!

Crusty Canadian White Bread

Ingredients:

- **For the Dough:**
    - 1 1/2 cups (360 ml) warm water (110°F/45°C)
    - 2 teaspoons (6 g) granulated sugar
    - 2 1/4 teaspoons (7 g) active dry yeast
    - 4 cups (500 g) all-purpose flour
    - 1 1/2 teaspoons (9 g) salt
    - 2 tablespoons (30 ml) olive oil or melted butter
- **For the Topping (optional):**
    - 1 tablespoon (15 ml) water
    - 1 tablespoon (15 g) all-purpose flour
    - 1 tablespoon (15 g) coarse sea salt or flaky sea salt

Instructions:

1. **Activate the Yeast:**
    - In a large bowl, combine the warm water and granulated sugar. Sprinkle the yeast over the top and let it sit for about 5-10 minutes, or until it becomes frothy.
2. **Prepare the Dough:**
    - Add the olive oil (or melted butter) to the yeast mixture and stir to combine.
    - In another bowl, whisk together the all-purpose flour and salt.
    - Gradually add the dry ingredients to the wet ingredients, mixing until a dough begins to form.
3. **Knead the Dough:**
    - Turn the dough out onto a floured surface and knead for about 8-10 minutes, or until smooth and elastic. You can also use a stand mixer with a dough hook attachment for this step.
4. **First Rise:**
    - Place the dough in a lightly oiled bowl, cover it with plastic wrap or a damp cloth, and let it rise in a warm place for about 1-1.5 hours, or until doubled in size.
5. **Shape the Loaf:**
    - Punch down the dough and turn it out onto a floured surface. Shape the dough into a loaf and place it in a greased 9x5 inch (23x13 cm) loaf pan or shape it into a round loaf and place it on a parchment-lined baking sheet.
6. **Second Rise:**
    - Cover the pan or loaf with a damp cloth and let it rise for another 30-45 minutes, or until it has risen significantly.
7. **Preheat Oven:**
    - Preheat your oven to 375°F (190°C).
8. **Prepare the Topping (Optional):**

- If using, mix the water and flour to make a thin paste. Brush the paste over the top of the loaf. Sprinkle with coarse sea salt or flaky sea salt for added texture and flavor.

9. **Bake the Bread:**
    - Bake in the preheated oven for 30-35 minutes, or until the bread is golden brown and sounds hollow when tapped on the bottom. The internal temperature should be around 190°F (88°C).
10. **Cool:**
    - Allow the bread to cool in the pan for about 10 minutes before transferring it to a wire rack to cool completely.

Notes:

- **Crust Variations:** For an extra-crispy crust, place a small oven-safe dish of water on the bottom rack of the oven while baking. The steam helps to develop a crusty exterior.
- **Flour:** Ensure that you use all-purpose flour for the best results. Bread flour can be used if you prefer a chewier texture.
- **Storage:** Store the cooled bread in an airtight container or plastic bag at room temperature for up to 4 days. It can also be frozen for up to 3 months. To refresh, let it thaw at room temperature or warm it slightly in the oven.

Enjoy your homemade Crusty Canadian White Bread, a perfect combination of a crispy crust and a soft, airy crumb!

Oat and Wheat Sandwich Bread

Ingredients:

- **For the Dough:**
    - 1 1/2 cups (360 ml) warm water (110°F/45°C)
    - 1/4 cup (60 ml) honey or maple syrup
    - 2 1/4 teaspoons (7 g) active dry yeast
    - 1 cup (90 g) old-fashioned rolled oats
    - 2 cups (250 g) whole wheat flour
    - 1 1/2 cups (190 g) all-purpose flour
    - 1/4 cup (30 g) wheat bran (optional, for extra fiber)
    - 1 teaspoon (5 g) salt
    - 1/4 cup (60 ml) olive oil or melted butter
- **For the Topping (optional):**
    - 2 tablespoons (15 g) old-fashioned rolled oats
    - 1 tablespoon (15 ml) water

Instructions:

1. **Prepare the Yeast Mixture:**
    - In a large bowl, combine the warm water and honey (or maple syrup). Sprinkle the yeast over the top and let it sit for about 5-10 minutes, or until it becomes frothy.
2. **Prepare the Oats:**
    - In a separate bowl, combine the rolled oats with 1/2 cup (120 ml) of hot water. Let them sit for about 10 minutes to soften.
3. **Mix the Dough:**
    - Add the softened oats, olive oil (or melted butter), and salt to the yeast mixture. Stir to combine.
    - In another bowl, whisk together the whole wheat flour, all-purpose flour, and wheat bran (if using).
    - Gradually add the dry ingredients to the wet ingredients, mixing until a dough forms.
4. **Knead the Dough:**
    - Turn the dough out onto a floured surface and knead for about 8-10 minutes, or until smooth and elastic. You can also use a stand mixer with a dough hook attachment for this step.
5. **First Rise:**
    - Place the dough in a lightly oiled bowl, cover it with plastic wrap or a damp cloth, and let it rise in a warm place for about 1 hour, or until doubled in size.
6. **Shape the Loaf:**

- Punch down the dough and turn it out onto a floured surface. Shape it into a loaf and place it in a greased 9x5 inch (23x13 cm) loaf pan.

7. **Second Rise:**
   - Cover the pan with a damp cloth or plastic wrap and let the dough rise for another 30-45 minutes, or until it has risen significantly.
8. **Preheat Oven:**
   - Preheat your oven to 375°F (190°C).
9. **Prepare the Topping (Optional):**
   - If using, mix the 2 tablespoons of rolled oats with 1 tablespoon of water to make a paste. Brush the paste over the top of the loaf for added texture and a rustic appearance.
10. **Bake the Bread:**
    - Bake in the preheated oven for 30-35 minutes, or until the bread is golden brown and sounds hollow when tapped on the bottom. The internal temperature should be around 190°F (88°C).
11. **Cool:**
    - Allow the bread to cool in the pan for about 10 minutes before transferring it to a wire rack to cool completely.

Notes:

- **Oats:** For added texture and flavor, you can use a mix of old-fashioned rolled oats and quick oats.
- **Wheat Bran:** Wheat bran adds extra fiber and a slightly nutty flavor but can be omitted if desired.
- **Storage:** Store the cooled bread in an airtight container or plastic bag at room temperature for up to 4 days. It can also be frozen for up to 3 months. To refresh, let it thaw at room temperature or warm it slightly in the oven.

Enjoy your homemade Oat and Wheat Sandwich Bread, a nutritious and hearty choice for any meal!

Cheddar and Jalapeno Bread

Ingredients:

- **For the Dough:**
    - 1 1/2 cups (360 ml) warm water (110°F/45°C)
    - 2 teaspoons (6 g) granulated sugar
    - 2 1/4 teaspoons (7 g) active dry yeast
    - 3 1/2 cups (440 g) all-purpose flour
    - 1 1/2 teaspoons (9 g) salt
    - 1 cup (115 g) sharp cheddar cheese, shredded
    - 2-3 fresh jalapeños, finely chopped (seeds removed for less heat)
    - 2 tablespoons (30 ml) olive oil or melted butter
- **For the Topping (optional):**
    - 1/2 cup (60 g) sharp cheddar cheese, shredded
    - 1-2 fresh jalapeños, thinly sliced (seeds removed for less heat)

Instructions:

1. **Prepare the Yeast Mixture:**
    - In a large bowl, combine the warm water and granulated sugar. Sprinkle the yeast over the top and let it sit for about 5-10 minutes, or until it becomes frothy.
2. **Mix the Dough:**
    - Add the olive oil (or melted butter) to the yeast mixture and stir to combine.
    - In another bowl, whisk together the all-purpose flour and salt.
    - Gradually add the dry ingredients to the wet ingredients, mixing until a dough forms.
    - Fold in the shredded cheddar cheese and chopped jalapeños.
3. **Knead the Dough:**
    - Turn the dough out onto a floured surface and knead for about 8-10 minutes, or until smooth and elastic. You can also use a stand mixer with a dough hook attachment for this step.
4. **First Rise:**
    - Place the dough in a lightly oiled bowl, cover it with plastic wrap or a damp cloth, and let it rise in a warm place for about 1 hour, or until doubled in size.
5. **Shape the Loaf:**
    - Punch down the dough and turn it out onto a floured surface. Shape it into a loaf and place it in a greased 9x5 inch (23x13 cm) loaf pan.
6. **Second Rise:**
    - Cover the pan with a damp cloth or plastic wrap and let the dough rise for another 30-45 minutes, or until it has risen significantly.
7. **Preheat Oven:**
    - Preheat your oven to 375°F (190°C).

8. **Prepare the Topping (Optional):**
   - If using, sprinkle the top of the loaf with the additional shredded cheddar cheese and arrange the thinly sliced jalapeños on top for added texture and flavor.
9. **Bake the Bread:**
   - Bake in the preheated oven for 30-35 minutes, or until the bread is golden brown and sounds hollow when tapped on the bottom. The internal temperature should be around 190°F (88°C).
10. **Cool:**
    - Allow the bread to cool in the pan for about 10 minutes before transferring it to a wire rack to cool completely.

Notes:

- **Cheddar Cheese:** Use a sharp cheddar for a more intense flavor, but feel free to use mild cheddar if you prefer a subtler taste.
- **Jalapeños:** Adjust the amount of jalapeños based on your heat preference. Removing the seeds will reduce the heat, while leaving them in will make the bread spicier.
- **Storage:** Store the cooled bread in an airtight container or plastic bag at room temperature for up to 4 days. It can also be frozen for up to 3 months. To refresh, let it thaw at room temperature or warm it slightly in the oven.

Enjoy your homemade Cheddar and Jalapeño Bread, a flavorful loaf that's sure to be a hit with anyone who enjoys a bit of spice!

Maple Apple Cinnamon Bread

Ingredients:

- **For the Dough:**
    - 1 cup (240 ml) warm milk (110°F/45°C)
    - 1/4 cup (60 ml) maple syrup
    - 2 1/4 teaspoons (7 g) active dry yeast
    - 1/2 cup (115 g) unsalted butter, softened
    - 2 large eggs
    - 4 cups (500 g) all-purpose flour
    - 1 teaspoon (5 g) salt
    - 1 teaspoon (5 g) ground cinnamon
- **For the Apple Filling:**
    - 1 large apple, peeled, cored, and finely diced
    - 1/4 cup (50 g) granulated sugar
    - 1 teaspoon (5 g) ground cinnamon
- **For the Maple Glaze (optional):**
    - 1/4 cup (60 ml) maple syrup
    - 1 cup (120 g) powdered sugar

Instructions:

1. **Prepare the Yeast Mixture:**
    - In a large bowl, combine the warm milk and maple syrup. Sprinkle the yeast over the top and let it sit for about 5-10 minutes, or until it becomes frothy.
2. **Mix the Dough:**
    - Add the softened butter and eggs to the yeast mixture and stir to combine.
    - In another bowl, whisk together the all-purpose flour, salt, and ground cinnamon.
    - Gradually add the dry ingredients to the wet ingredients, mixing until a dough forms.
3. **Knead the Dough:**
    - Turn the dough out onto a floured surface and knead for about 8-10 minutes, or until smooth and elastic. You can also use a stand mixer with a dough hook attachment for this step.
4. **First Rise:**
    - Place the dough in a lightly oiled bowl, cover it with plastic wrap or a damp cloth, and let it rise in a warm place for about 1 hour, or until doubled in size.
5. **Prepare the Apple Filling:**
    - In a small bowl, combine the diced apple with granulated sugar and ground cinnamon. Set aside.
6. **Shape the Loaf:**

- Punch down the dough and turn it out onto a floured surface. Roll the dough into a rectangle about 1/4 inch (6 mm) thick.
- Evenly sprinkle the apple mixture over the dough, leaving a small border around the edges. Roll the dough tightly into a log.

7. **Second Rise:**
    - Place the rolled dough seam-side down in a greased 9x5 inch (23x13 cm) loaf pan. Cover with a damp cloth or plastic wrap and let it rise for another 30-45 minutes, or until it has risen significantly.
8. **Preheat Oven:**
    - Preheat your oven to 350°F (175°C).
9. **Bake the Bread:**
    - Bake in the preheated oven for 35-40 minutes, or until the bread is golden brown and sounds hollow when tapped on the bottom. The internal temperature should be around 190°F (88°C).
10. **Prepare the Maple Glaze (Optional):**
    - While the bread is baking, whisk together the maple syrup and powdered sugar until smooth.
11. **Cool and Glaze:**
    - Allow the bread to cool in the pan for about 10 minutes before transferring it to a wire rack.
    - If desired, drizzle the maple glaze over the warm bread once it has cooled slightly.

Notes:

- **Apple Type:** Use a firm apple variety such as Granny Smith or Honeycrisp for the best texture and flavor.
- **Maple Glaze:** The glaze adds extra sweetness and a touch of maple flavor, but it can be omitted if you prefer a less sweet bread.
- **Storage:** Store the cooled bread in an airtight container or plastic bag at room temperature for up to 4 days. It can also be frozen for up to 3 months. To refresh, let it thaw at room temperature or warm it slightly in the oven.

Enjoy your homemade Maple Apple Cinnamon Bread, a sweet and comforting loaf that's perfect for any occasion!

Flavored Bannock Bread

Ingredients:

- **For the Dough:**
    - 2 cups (250 g) all-purpose flour
    - 1 tablespoon (15 g) granulated sugar
    - 1 tablespoon (15 g) baking powder
    - 1/2 teaspoon (3 g) salt
    - 1/2 cup (115 g) cold butter, cubed
    - 3/4 cup (180 ml) milk (or buttermilk for a tangier flavor)
    - 1 large egg
- **For Flavor Variations:**
    - **Herb Bannock:**
        - 2 tablespoons (6 g) dried mixed herbs (such as rosemary, thyme, and oregano)
    - **Cheddar and Chive Bannock:**
        - 1 cup (115 g) shredded cheddar cheese
        - 1/4 cup (10 g) chopped fresh chives
    - **Spicy Jalapeño Bannock:**
        - 1/4 cup (30 g) finely chopped fresh jalapeños (seeds removed for less heat)
        - 1 teaspoon (5 g) ground cumin
    - **Sweet Berry Bannock:**
        - 1 cup (140 g) fresh or frozen berries (such as blueberries or raspberries)
        - 1 teaspoon (5 g) ground cinnamon

Instructions:

1. **Prepare the Dry Ingredients:**
    - In a large bowl, whisk together the all-purpose flour, granulated sugar, baking powder, and salt.
2. **Cut in the Butter:**
    - Add the cold butter cubes to the dry ingredients. Using a pastry cutter or your fingers, cut the butter into the flour mixture until it resembles coarse crumbs.
3. **Mix the Wet Ingredients:**
    - In a separate bowl, whisk together the milk (or buttermilk) and egg.
4. **Combine Ingredients:**
    - Pour the wet ingredients into the dry ingredients and stir until just combined. The dough will be slightly sticky.
5. **Add Flavorings:**
    - If using, gently fold in the desired flavorings (herbs, cheese, chives, jalapeños, cumin, berries, or cinnamon).

6. **Prepare for Baking:**
   - Turn the dough out onto a floured surface and shape it into a round disc about 1-inch (2.5 cm) thick. If the dough is too sticky, you can flour your hands or the surface lightly.
7. **Cook the Bannock:**
   - **Skillet Method:** Heat a skillet or frying pan over medium heat. Lightly grease the skillet with butter or oil. Cook the bannock in the skillet for 8-10 minutes on each side, or until golden brown and cooked through.
   - **Oven Method:** Preheat your oven to 375°F (190°C). Place the shaped dough on a baking sheet lined with parchment paper. Bake for 20-25 minutes, or until the bannock is golden brown and a toothpick inserted into the center comes out clean.
8. **Cool:**
   - Allow the bannock to cool slightly before slicing. It can be enjoyed warm or at room temperature.

Notes:

- **Flavor Combinations:** Feel free to get creative with additional flavorings like nuts, seeds, dried fruits, or spices.
- **Texture:** For a softer texture, add a bit more milk or buttermilk. For a denser texture, you can use less liquid.
- **Storage:** Store leftover bannock in an airtight container at room temperature for up to 3 days. It can also be frozen for up to 2 months. To refresh, let it thaw at room temperature or warm it slightly in the oven.

Enjoy your homemade Flavored Bannock Bread, perfect for a hearty breakfast, a delicious snack, or a unique addition to any meal!

Wild Mushroom Rye Bread

Ingredients:

- **For the Dough:**
    - 1 1/2 cups (360 ml) warm water (110°F/45°C)
    - 2 teaspoons (6 g) granulated sugar
    - 2 1/4 teaspoons (7 g) active dry yeast
    - 1 cup (120 g) rye flour
    - 2 cups (250 g) all-purpose flour
    - 1 teaspoon (5 g) salt
    - 1 tablespoon (15 ml) caraway seeds (optional, for traditional rye flavor)
    - 1/4 cup (60 ml) olive oil
- **For the Wild Mushroom Filling:**
    - 1 cup (100 g) wild mushrooms, finely chopped (such as shiitake, porcini, or oyster)
    - 1 tablespoon (15 ml) olive oil
    - 1 small onion, finely chopped
    - 2 cloves garlic, minced
    - 1/4 teaspoon (1 g) dried thyme
    - Salt and pepper to taste

Instructions:

1. **Prepare the Yeast Mixture:**
    - In a large bowl, combine the warm water and granulated sugar. Sprinkle the yeast over the top and let it sit for about 5-10 minutes, or until it becomes frothy.
2. **Prepare the Wild Mushroom Filling:**
    - Heat 1 tablespoon of olive oil in a skillet over medium heat. Add the finely chopped onion and cook until translucent, about 5 minutes.
    - Add the garlic and cook for an additional 1 minute.
    - Add the finely chopped mushrooms, dried thyme, salt, and pepper. Cook until the mushrooms are softened and the liquid has evaporated, about 7-10 minutes. Remove from heat and let cool.
3. **Mix the Dough:**
    - In a large bowl, whisk together the rye flour, all-purpose flour, salt, and caraway seeds (if using).
    - Gradually add the dry ingredients to the yeast mixture, mixing until a dough forms.
    - Stir in the olive oil and mix until incorporated.
4. **Knead the Dough:**

- Turn the dough out onto a floured surface and knead for about 8-10 minutes, or until smooth and elastic. You can also use a stand mixer with a dough hook attachment for this step.
5. **Incorporate the Mushroom Filling:**
    - Gently fold the cooled mushroom mixture into the dough until evenly distributed.
6. **First Rise:**
    - Place the dough in a lightly oiled bowl, cover it with plastic wrap or a damp cloth, and let it rise in a warm place for about 1 hour, or until doubled in size.
7. **Shape the Loaf:**
    - Punch down the dough and turn it out onto a floured surface. Shape it into a loaf and place it in a greased 9x5 inch (23x13 cm) loaf pan.
8. **Second Rise:**
    - Cover the pan with a damp cloth or plastic wrap and let the dough rise for another 30-45 minutes, or until it has risen significantly.
9. **Preheat Oven:**
    - Preheat your oven to 375°F (190°C).
10. **Bake the Bread:**
    - Bake in the preheated oven for 35-40 minutes, or until the bread is golden brown and sounds hollow when tapped on the bottom. The internal temperature should be around 190°F (88°C).
11. **Cool:**
    - Allow the bread to cool in the pan for about 10 minutes before transferring it to a wire rack to cool completely.

Notes:

- **Mushroom Varieties:** Use a mix of wild mushrooms for a richer flavor. If wild mushrooms are unavailable, you can substitute with common varieties like button or cremini mushrooms.
- **Texture:** The rye flour adds a dense, hearty texture. For a lighter loaf, you can substitute part of the rye flour with more all-purpose flour.
- **Storage:** Store the cooled bread in an airtight container or plastic bag at room temperature for up to 4 days. It can also be frozen for up to 3 months. To refresh, let it thaw at room temperature or warm it slightly in the oven.

Enjoy your Wild Mushroom Rye Bread, a savory and satisfying loaf that's perfect for sandwiches, toasts, or simply enjoyed with a pat of butter!

Vancouver Island Gingerbread

Ingredients:

- **For the Gingerbread:**
    - 2 1/4 cups (280 g) all-purpose flour
    - 1 teaspoon (5 g) baking powder
    - 1/2 teaspoon (2 g) baking soda
    - 1/2 teaspoon (2 g) salt
    - 1 tablespoon (8 g) ground ginger
    - 1 tablespoon (8 g) ground cinnamon
    - 1/2 teaspoon (2 g) ground cloves
    - 1/2 teaspoon (2 g) ground nutmeg
    - 1/2 cup (115 g) unsalted butter, softened
    - 1/2 cup (100 g) granulated sugar
    - 1/2 cup (120 ml) molasses
    - 1 large egg
    - 1/2 cup (120 ml) hot water
- **For the Glaze (optional):**
    - 1/2 cup (60 g) powdered sugar
    - 1 tablespoon (15 ml) milk or water
    - 1/4 teaspoon (1 g) vanilla extract

Instructions:

1. **Preheat Oven:**
    - Preheat your oven to 350°F (175°C). Grease and flour a 9x5 inch (23x13 cm) loaf pan or line it with parchment paper.
2. **Prepare the Dry Ingredients:**
    - In a medium bowl, whisk together the all-purpose flour, baking powder, baking soda, salt, ground ginger, ground cinnamon, ground cloves, and ground nutmeg. Set aside.
3. **Cream the Butter and Sugar:**
    - In a large bowl, use an electric mixer to cream together the softened butter and granulated sugar until light and fluffy.
4. **Add Molasses and Egg:**
    - Beat in the molasses and then the egg, mixing well after each addition.
5. **Combine Dry and Wet Ingredients:**
    - Gradually add the dry ingredients to the wet ingredients, mixing until just combined.
    - Stir in the hot water until the batter is smooth.
6. **Pour and Bake:**
    - Pour the batter into the prepared loaf pan and smooth the top with a spatula.

- Bake in the preheated oven for 50-60 minutes, or until a toothpick inserted into the center comes out clean and the top is golden brown.

7. **Cool:**
    - Allow the gingerbread to cool in the pan for about 10 minutes before transferring it to a wire rack to cool completely.

8. **Prepare the Glaze (Optional):**
    - While the bread is cooling, prepare the glaze by whisking together the powdered sugar, milk or water, and vanilla extract until smooth.
    - Drizzle the glaze over the cooled gingerbread.

Notes:

- **Flavor Variations:** You can add a pinch of black pepper for an extra kick or mix in some chopped candied ginger for added texture.
- **Texture:** The molasses and spices give the gingerbread a rich, moist texture. If you prefer a less dense bread, you can substitute part of the all-purpose flour with cake flour.
- **Storage:** Store the cooled gingerbread in an airtight container at room temperature for up to 1 week. It can also be frozen for up to 3 months. To refresh, let it thaw at room temperature or warm it slightly in the oven.

Enjoy your Vancouver Island Gingerbread, a delightful and aromatic bread that's perfect for any time of year!